D1106419

ca. 1860

ST.PAUL

ST.PAUL

Saga of an American City

Virginia Brainard Kunz

*Published under
the sponsorship of the
St. Paul Area Chamber of Commerce.
Research and editorial
supervision provided by
the Ramsey County Historical Society,
Robert Orr Baker, Research Director.*

WINDSOR PUBLICATIONS, INC./WOODLAND HILLS, CALIF.

Copyright© 1977, Windsor Publications, Inc.

PRINTED IN THE UNITED STATES OF AMERICA

Executive Design Director/Cal Freedman

Designer/A.B. Mifflin

*To those who
have unselfishly given
freely of themselves in the
unfolding of the saga
of St. Paul.*

*. . . The history of
the world is but
the biography of
great men.*

CARLYLE

Contents

ACKNOWLEDGMENTS

This book owes its existence to a widely shared interest in the history of St. Paul on the part of its people, among them the members of the St. Paul Area Chamber of Commerce who asked the Ramsey County Historical Society to join with them in producing the first history of St. Paul in more than sixty years.

But any history that reflects, as this does, the lives of thousands of people over a hundred and more years is never the work of one person. Major responsibility for the book's manuscript was assumed by the Society's Publications Committee: Robert Orr Baker, chairman; Dr. Rodney C. Loehr, professor emeritus of history, University of Minnesota; Dr. Ernest R. Sandeen, professor of history, Macalester College; Professor Thomas C. Buckley, chairman of the Department of Social and Behavioral Sciences, University of Minnesota; and Al Rung. Committee members patiently read through several drafts of the manuscript, and made valuable suggestions and corrections.

Staff researchers Anne Cowie and Peggy Korsmo Kennon combed the magnificent picture collections at the Minnesota Historical Society, the Minneapolis and St. Paul Public Libraries, the Hill Reference Library, and the library at the St. Paul *Dispatch* and *Pioneer Press*, and also extracted information "on demand" from research in the Minnesota Historical Society and the Ramsey County Historical Society collections.

Society staff members Judy Osborn and Annette Calhoun copied hundreds of pages of manuscript. And free-lance writer Carol Pine researched and wrote the business biographies which contribute significantly to the interest of the book.

The Saint Paul Foundation, the Bigelow Foundation, the Bush Foundation, and the Minnesota Bicentennial Commission, under its chairman Governor Rudy Perpich, generously granted funds to the Ramsey County Historical Society for exhibitions and publications that made it possible for the Society to amass a body of research on the remarkable and colorful history of the city and county.

Throughout the past year, the Ramsey County Historical Society's Board of Directors has provided enthusiastic approval and support for this project. Richard T. Murphy, president, directs the volunteer efforts of his fellow board members: Robert B. Mirick, Mrs. Stanley J. Fiorito, Jr., James Stolpestad, Mrs. Joseph North, James Russell, Robert Orr Baker, John M. Baker, George Bohrer, Thomas C. Buckley, Wayne Burlingame, Mrs. John Costello, Anthony DeZiel, Richard T. Faricy, Joseph L. Fox, Mrs. Gale Frost, Henry Hall, William Kircher, Frank Paskewitz, John Rockney, John Brown, Clyde Reedy, Ernest Sandeen, Dewan Barnes, and Leonard Levine.

The Ramsey County Board of Commissioners — Warren W. Schaber, chairman; Donald Salverda; Hal Norgard; John T. Finley; Diane Ahrens; Anthony Dana; and Robert J. Orth — provide continuing support for the Society's work and deserve its gratitude.

Finally, and most important, the St. Paul Area Chamber of Commerce deserves the credit for making this book possible, and particularly Roy Svee, the Chamber's president; John Verstraete, vice president, Social Action Group; co-vice-chairmen, Project Responsibility, Howard Dalton and John Mason; A. Kent Shamblin, chairman, Corporate Social Responsibility Committee; Andy Czajkowski, chairman, Arts and Cultural Task Force; Wilbur Bush; Arnold Niemeyer; William West; Amos Martin, executive vice president, St. Paul Area Chamber of Commerce; and Bill Nelson, manager of the Social Action Group.

In the last analysis, the writing of history is a matter of selection, more than anything else, and for that any writer must stand accountable. No history, moreover, can trace every detail in the infinite number of details that are part of a long historical record, and, particularly in the writing of a short history, the agonizing problem of what has to be left out becomes particularly acute. For this we beg sympathy, if not complete acceptance of our decisions.

V.B.K.

A

Part One/Trappers, Traders, and the Settling of St. Paul

To the Indians it was *Im-in-i-ja Ska*, or White Rock — the sweep of white sandstone bluffs eighty feet high that follows the curve of the Mississippi and, unchanged through thousands of years, still marks the site of St. Paul.

For centuries, the Indian bands were simply passing through the region in hunting or war parties, or on pilgrimages to what is now Indian Mounds Park. They did not establish permanent villages in the St. Paul area until late in the 18th century, so that when the first Europeans arrived 100 years earlier, they found a migratory people, the Mdewakanton or "river bands" of the Sioux, camping there.

About 1775 the Kaposia band, under Chief Little Crow, settled at the "Grand Marais," the nearly forgotten French name for "the hay meadows," the marshy area down the river now called "Pig's Eye." Lieutenant Zebulon Pike found the village there in the summer of 1805 when he came upriver from St. Louis to explore the upper reaches of the Mississippi, and he also noted a "Camp of Four Lodges" at the mouth of what is now Phalen Creek.

By the early 1820s, the Kaposia band also had moved to the mouth of the creek, and it remained there until 1833 when it finally came to rest at present-day South St. Paul, near the stockyards.

More than a century before Pike's expedition, intense interest in the upper Mississippi had been aroused by a colorful account of an extraordinary trip written by the first European to arrive in the St. Paul area. Father Louis Hennepin, a Franciscan with a passion for adventure, joined La Salle's expedition from Canada into the Illinois country. In February, 1680, La Salle sent Hennepin and two other men to explore the northern stretch of the Mississippi.

According to *Description de la Louisiane*, which Hennepin published three years later, the men encountered a war party of Sioux who either invited them, or insisted that they accompany them, up the

A *Little Crow, hereditary successor to the chieftainship of the Kaposia band of the Sioux.*

1

A

river. On April 30, 1680, the Indians and their "guests" landed at an inlet "five leagues below the Falls of Saint Anthony," a place overgrown with rushes and a location generally believed to be the little bay at the Phalen Creek outlet. Later that year Hennepin discovered and christened the Falls of St. Anthony.

Hennepin's account was the first known written description of the region surrounding St. Paul. In the next six years, Nicholas Perrot, a French officer, built a fort on Lake Pepin to anchor a network of fur trading posts. With him came Pierre Charles Le Sueur and Rene Boucher, Sieur de la Perriere, and their canoes and men swept back and forth along the great bend of the Mississippi past the site of St. Paul to the mouth of the St. Peter (Minnesota) River. They were the region's first entrepreneurs, engaged in the strictly organized and closely supervised fur business that eventually became a mainstay of St. Paul's economic life and did not disappear until the 1930s.

In 1765, following the French and Indian War, the British took control of the area. A year later, Jonathan Carver, the last of those romantic explorers who were bemused by visions of a Northwest Passage, arrived to explore the upper Mississippi region. He discovered one of St. Paul's most enduring historic sites, Carver's Cave, in the sandstone bluffs below Indian Mounds Park. In his book, *Travels Through the Interior Parts of North America*, he described it as, "a remarkable cave of amazing depth."

B

The Indians, he wrote, "term it *Wakan-Teebe*, that is, 'The Dwelling of the Great Spirit.' The entrance into it is about ten feet wide, and the height of it five feet." The bottom, he said, was of fine sand; there was a clear, deep lake in its interior and Indian hieroglyphics, covered with moss, adorned the walls.

Carver reported that the cave was reached only by "a narrow, steep passage that lies near the brink of the river." Today the cave is not accessible at all. Its face was cut back by railroad construction, and its entrance blocked by rock slides from the overhanging bluffs.

During the next fifty some years, the British, who had taken over the French fur posts, established their own posts and, despite such upheavals as the

C

D

American Revolution, did not relinquish control of the region until after the War of 1812.
About 130 known trading posts were scattered throughout Minnesota.

The Indians were the partners of these adventurous traders, exchanging pelts for arms, ammunition, blankets, and beads, and joining them as allies during the American Revolution. The Sioux Chief Wabasha, then living in the St. Paul area, and the Chippewa Chief Matchekewis, joined the British in recruiting 750 Indians and traders for an attack on St. Louis. The city was held by the Spanish, who had entered the war on the American side in 1779. Wabasha had been given a British general's commission and uniform, and he led a force of 200 Santee Sioux warriors.

A *Wabasha's village on the Mississippi, 1846-1848, one of Seth Eastman's delightful watercolors.*
B *Lieutenant Zebulon Pike, an oil portrait by an unknown artist.*
C *"The Falls of St. Anthony As It Appeared in 1848." Henry Lewis painted this oil in 1855.*
D *Father Louis Hennepin, about 1694, when his account of his travels was a best-seller in Europe. The artist is unknown.*

The attack, known as the "coup d'annee," took place May 26, 1780. It was repulsed by the Spanish, and Wabasha and his warriors retreated to Prairie du Chien, but the incident remains an interesting footnote to history, and the only known involvement in the Revolution by men living in what is now Minnesota.

A

B

WAH-PA-SHA
CHIEF OF SIOUX

C

A *Forbes Trading Post, operated by W.H. Forbes for the Indian trade in 1847 at Fifth and Robert streets. (Sketch by R.O. Sweeny.)*

B *View of Fort Snelling, about 1850, an oil by Sergeant Edward K. Thomas.*

C *Wabasha, Sioux Chief and acknowledged leader of the seven Sioux bands in the St. Paul area, who led the attack on St. Louis on May 26, 1780, remembered as the "coup d'annee."*

D *Jonathan Carver, who reached the site of present-day St. Paul in 1766 and held a council with the Sioux in the great cave which bears his name at Dayton's Bluff.*

Capt. JONATHAN CARVER.

D

In 1803 the Louisiana Purchase brought all of the St. Paul area into American hands. The region had belonged to five separate governments. St. Paul's West Side was Spanish territory and ceded, not long before the Louisiana Purchase, to the France of Napoleon. St. Paul itself stands on territory that belonged to the France of the monarchy, and then to the British, before passing to the Americans.

In 1805 General James Wilkinson, military governor of upper Louisiana, assigned Pike to explore the region drained by the upper Mississippi and to break the British monopoly on the fur trade. Almost as an afterthought, he directed Pike to treat with the Indians for land for a military post.

By September 22 Pike had set up camp on the island that has been named for him, and begun talks with the Mdewakanton chiefs. Among others present was Robert Dickson, a red-headed Scotsman who, as chief factor in the region for the North West Fur Company, had great influence with the Sioux. He controlled fur posts from the St. Paul area to the Red River.

In an agreement signed by Little Crow, Pike acquired nine square miles of land surrounding the junction of the Minnesota and Mississippi rivers. For the next fifteen years, however, the British traders remained in control of the region. During the War of 1812, Dickson, whose sympathies were ardently British, enlisted bands of Indians, including the Mdewakanton, for attacks that captured Fort Mackinac on Mackinac Island and Fort Shelby at Prairie du Chien for the British. But at the end of the war, the British traders recognized the inevitable. Through the simple expedient of becoming American citizens, they did business as usual with the Mdewakanton.

The United States now moved to build a fort on the land Pike had purchased. Aware of the fuzziness of the Canadian boundary and of the bitter warfare between the two rival Canadian fur companies, the North West Company and the Hudson's Bay Company, the Americans also wished to keep an eye on the Selkirk Colony at Fort Garry, near present-day Winnipeg. Supply caravans for Fort Garry were being routed through Minnesota.

In 1819 Lieutenant Colonel Henry Leavenworth and a detachment of men from the Fifth United States Infantry began the construction of Fort Snelling. In 1821 the first refugees from the Selkirk Colony arrived to settle as squatters on land just outside the fort. A quarter of a century later, they became the first settlers of St. Paul.

The Selkirk Colony had been founded in 1812 by a Scottish nobleman, Thomas Douglas, the Earl of Selkirk. He had a somewhat Utopian dream of providing homes for poor immigrants who would grow food for Hudson's Bay Company traders. A large stockholder in the company, Selkirk secured an immense tract of land at the junction of the Red and Assiniboine rivers and colonized the region with Scottish crofters and Swiss artisans. The colony was beset by disasters. Grasshoppers and mice devoured the crops, the cold froze both the crops and the colonists, disastrous floods on the Assiniboine destroyed their homes and food, the warring fur companies were a constant danger, and the Sioux of the Prairies terrified the settlers.

Five families, discouraged by the Selkirk venture, journeyed south to Fort Snelling where the fort's commandant, Colonel Josiah Snelling, allowed them to establish small farms on the military reservation. In 1823 thirteen more families came, and in 1826, 243 colonists arrived, most of them Swiss. There were other settlers around the fort. Among them were a number of traders who were working for Henry H. Sibley, the American Fur Company's agent at

---

... the most beastly scenes of intoxication among the soldiers ... and the Indians

---

Mendota. There also were the *bois-brulés*, half-breed French voyageurs who had retired from the fur trade, and several discharged soldiers.

Toward the end of the 1830s, relations between officers and civilians became strained. The post command was concerned about dwindling supplies of forage and fuel, with both soldiers and settlers pasturing cattle and cutting timber on the same land. A more emotional and dramatic issue was the sale of whiskey to soldiers and Indians by traders operating shops across the river from the fort in what is now Highland Park.

"Since the middle of winter," the fort's surgeon wrote in April, 1839, "we have been completely inundated with ardent spirits, and consequently the most beastly scenes of intoxication among the soldiers of this garrison and the Indians in its vicinity, which no doubt will add many cases to our sick list . . . ." On June 3, 1839, forty-seven soldiers were in the guardhouse after a riotous spree in a dram shop across the river.

In 1837 treaties with the Sioux and Chippewa opened to settlement a wide tract of land from the east bank of the Mississippi to the St. Croix River. The tract embraced the site of St. Paul. A survey that autumn revealed that 157 persons not connected with the fort were living on the military reservation.

To Major Joseph Plympton, the fort's new commander, the presence of these civilians was irritating. He decided that formal boundaries should be drawn for the military reservation and he indicated that no civilians would be allowed to cut timber, or erect buildings and fences on the newly established reservation.

Realizing that they no longer were welcome on the military reservation, several families moved down the Mississippi and staked the first formal claims to land in what is now St. Paul. Believing they were beyond the bounds of the reservation, they built new homes around Fountain Cave on the east bank of the river between present-day Barton and Randolph streets. Among them were a French-Canadian voyageur named Pierre "Pig's Eye" Parrant and a Swiss watchmaker named Abraham Perry or Perret, who generally have been regarded as the first settlers of St. Paul.

That honor, however, does not belong to them. For some years before the little settlement was established at Fountain Cave, a number of other men had been living within the present city limits of St. Paul, on the east side of the Mississippi in the area extending from present-day Marshall Avenue through Highland Park to the river. They included Joseph Turpin, Francis Desire, Donald McDonald, and "Old Man" Chorette.

J. Fletcher Williams, who wrote the liveliest of the old histories of St. Paul, believes that Turpin was the first man to build a house on the east bank of the river in what is now St. Paul. Both Turpin, who was born in Montreal, Canada, about 1775, and Chorette moved to the fort from the Selkirk Colony about 1831. Desire, who seems to have had a colorful background in Napoleon's army, had been a soldier at Fort Snelling.

McDonald, a Scotsman, was born in Canada in 1803 and had worked for the American Fur Company. He may have built the third house on the east bank. His cabin, near the present site of the Town and Country Club, was a grog shop known as the "Halfway House" — halfway between Fort Snelling and the Falls of St. Anthony. *The Glaucus*, the first steamboat to land in what is now St. Paul, stopped at his establishment on May 21, 1839, to unload six barrels of whiskey. In 1845 McDonald sold his 320-acre claim to Stephen Desnoyer, who carried on the "Halfway House" name and tradition with a saloon and hotel on the site of the Shriners Hospital.

But it is on Parrant, in particular, that the mantle of first settler, even founder, of St. Paul has settled, due perhaps to Williams' gift for whimsy in the writing of history — a warning that historians who write tongue-in-cheek may encourage future generations to believe them. Parrant was one of those interesting characters with which Western history is sprinkled. By the 1830s he was about 60 years old and had abandoned or been cast out of the fur trade. He had lived both at Sault Ste. Marie and St. Louis where he had been employed by the fur traders McKenzie and Chouteau. The Indian agent at Fort Snelling, Lawrence Taliaferro, had such a low opinion of him that, as he noted in his journal for August 23, 1835, he had ordered Parrant, "a foreigner, prohibited from the [fur] trade, not to enter Indian country in any capacity."

Parrant's personal appearance did nothing to inspire trust. Williams described him as a "coarse, ill-looking, low-browed fellow, with only one eye. He spoke execrable English. His habits were intemperate and licentious." His eye was "blind, marble-hued, crooked, with a sinister white ring glaring around the pupil, giving a kind of piggish expression to his sodden, low features." Parrant now proposed to set himself up as a whiskey-seller. About June 1, 1838, he built his cabin in the secluded gorge at the mouth of the stream that flows out of Fountain Cave.

His fellow settler there, Abraham Perry, was a very different sort of man. A refugee from the Selkirk Colony, he had been born in Switzerland about 1780, and had been a watchmaker. With his wife, three children, and a considerable number of his countrymen, he had emigrated to the Red River colony in 1820. He arrived at Fort Snelling in 1827, settled north of the fort near Camp Coldwater, opened a farm, and prospered. According to Colonel John H. Stevens, the first settler of Minneapolis, Perry owned more cattle than all the rest of the families, except for Joseph Renville, a fur trader who also lived on the military reservation.

The move to Fountain Cave was a cruel blow to Perry, who was no longer young. Settling with him and Parrant in the nine cabins clustered around the cave were, among others, Pierre and Benjamin Gervais, also refugees from the Red River country.

Within a few months, however, the survey of the military reservation had been completed. To the dismay of the Fountain Cave settlers, Major Plympton had extended the reservation's eastern boundary beyond them to what is now Seven Corners in downtown St. Paul. Notice was given that they must move again. They refused. On May 6, 1840, they were evicted from their cabins by soldiers from the fort who carried out their household goods and destroyed their cabins. This time they moved to the site of the Lower Landing at the foot of Jackson Street, and there the permanent settlement of St. Paul took root. The ubiquitous Parrant was already in residence. He had lost his Fountain Cave claim in

A

C

B

A *Immigrants starting for the West. They were typical of the 30,000 or so new settlers who arrived in Minnesota in 1855.*

B *Vetal Guerin, an employee of the American Fur Company at Mendota, who settled on a claim in downtown St. Paul in 1840.*

C *Lawrence Taliaferro, Indian agent at Fort Snelling. The artist might have been George Catlin.*

A

May, 1839, and had set up shop on a new claim at the Lower Landing.

Even so, he was not the first man there. It was the Irish, not the French, who were the first to settle in downtown St. Paul. Edward Phelan, who was born in Londonderry and whose name is carried as "Felyn" on the army records, and John Hays, a native of Waterford, had been living there for a month on adjoining claims. Both had been discharged from the army at Fort Snelling.

Phelan's claim extended along the river flats from Eagle to St. Peter streets. He had built a cabin under the bluff, below today's Kellogg Boulevard.* Hays shared the cabin; his own claim extended from St. Peter to Minnesota streets, and from the river back to the bluff. A third discharged soldier and another native of Ireland, William Evans, was the first settler on Dayton's Bluff. He also had taken up his claim in 1839.

When Parrant joined Phelan and Hays, he selected land east of Hays' claim, from Minnesota to Jackson streets and from the river to the bluff. There, near the foot of Robert Street and on a rise of land, he built a hovel where he lived and ran his saloon.

The little settlement at the Lower Landing was nameless. Enter, one day in 1839, Edmund Brissette, a young Canadian doing odd carpentry, who wanted to send a letter to Joseph R. Brown on Grey Cloud Island. Brissette was stopping at Parrant's place and there he pondered the problem of where to date the letter.

"I looked up inquiringly at Parrant," he recalled, "and, seeing his old crooked eye scowling at me, it suddenly popped into my head to date it at 'Pig's Eye', feeling sure that the place would be recognized, as Parrant was well-known along the river. In a little while an answer was safely received, directed to me at Pig's Eye."

In 1844 Parrant moved to the Grand Marais and the name, Pig's Eye, has been attached to that location ever since. After a few months he sold his claim and started for Sault Ste. Marie, but died before reaching Lake Superior "of a disease," according to Williams, "resulting from his own vices."

---

*Kellogg Boulevard once was Third Street. To avoid repetition and confusion, this principal street of the early city will be referred to by its original name of Third Street up to 1928 and 1929 when the boulevard was created and the street renamed.

A   *Father Galtier's Chapel of St. Paul, an oil painted by R.O. Sweeny in 1852.*
B   *Father Lucien Galtier, an oil painted by Andrew Falkenshield about 1890.*
C   *James M. Goodhue, founder and editor of the* Minnesota Pioneer.

By this time the first marriage, the birth of the first white child, and the first death had taken place in St. Paul. James R. Clewett married Abraham Perry's daughter, Rose; Basil Gervais was born to Benjamin Gervais and his wife, and John Hays was murdered. His body was found in the river near Carver's Cave, his head bashed in.

Phelan, who had a reputation for cruelty, was arrested immediately and taken to Prairie du Chien for trial. The grand jury released him, however, for lack of evidence and sometime later a Sioux warrior confessed that he had killed Hays. Phelan returned to St. Paul and took up a new claim on the creek that bears his name (now spelled Phalen) near the present-day Olympia (formerly Hamm's) Brewery.

Most of the refugees from the military reservation now were settled in homes around the Lower Landing. Abraham Perry, much broken in health and spirit by being twice uprooted, found a home with James Clewett, and Benjamin Gervais bought Parrant's claim, today some of the most valuable real estate in St. Paul, for $10.

Vetal Guerin, a young Canadian voyageur who had turned to farming, took over Hays' claim. Then, feeling lonely and wanting a neighbor, he generously gave half of it to Pierre Gervais, Benjamin's brother. Joseph Rondo bought Phelan's

earlier claim, and Pierre Bottineau and his brother, Severe, secured a small tract of land on Baptist Hill from Benjamin Gervais.

In 1840 an earnest young priest had arrived to minister to the French-Canadians at Mendota and soon found he would have to follow his parishioners down the river. Father Lucien Galtier now needed a suitable site for a church. In an account written in 1864, he recalled that, "Mr. B. Gervais and Mr. Vetal Guerin, two good quiet farmers, had the only spot that appeared likely to answer the purpose. They consented to give me jointly the ground necessary for a church site, a garden and a small graveyard. I accepted the extreme eastern part of Mr. Vetal's claim, and the extreme west of Mr. Gervais'." Accordingly, in 1841, in the month of October, logs were prepared and a church erected, so poor that it would well remind one of the stable at Bethlehem. It was destined, however, to be the nucleus of a great city.

"On the 1st day of November, in the same year, I blessed the new basilica, and dedicated it to 'Saint Paul, the apostle of nations.' I expressed a wish, at the same time, that the settlement would be known by the same name, and my desire was obtained . . ."

James M. Goodhue, St. Paul's pioneer newspaper

editor, hailed the change of name in a "New Year's Address" of January 1, 1850:

"Pig's Eye, converted thou shalt be, like Saul;
Arise, and be, henceforth, Saint Paul!"

The site of St. Paul was not chosen entirely by accident, although its first settlers seem to have stumbled toward it. They knew, however, that this was the head of navigation on the upper Mississippi, and it was referred to as such in most of the early accounts of the region.

The hamlet was divided into two sections created by natural breaks in the bluffs crowning its spectacular site. The major landing site, and the first encountered by boats coming up the river, was at the foot of Jackson Street. This was the Lower Landing, variously called the Jackson Street Landing, Robert's Landing, and Lambert's Landing — all names of early merchants. The business and residential district that sprang up around the landing is still known today as Lower Town.

There was a second landing upstream, the Upper Landing at the foot of Chestnut and Eagle streets where steamboats plying the Minnesota River arrived and departed. It had its own business and residential district known as Upper Town — the Seven Corners area today. Separated from each other by the bluffs, the two sites were virtually separate communities and economic rivalry between them was intense.

The *Pioneer and Democrat*, in its issue for February 15, 1856, commented on one aspect of this mutual independence: "Great inconvenience has been experienced in St. Paul, owing to the want of Standard time. Usually, upper and lower town time differs five, ten, and even fifteen minutes, each section persisting in the correctness of its own regulator. To obviate the inconvenience . . . the council adopted a resolution . . . for the purpose of fixing upon some standard which will regulate time in different parts of the town."

A dense forest of elms surrounded the Upper Landing below Third Street, and along the base of Summit Hill were stands of cedar and tamarack. During the 1840s and 1850s a bog extended from

A

where the Minnesota Club is located today, north past Assumption Church and over to Seven Corners. A small stream ran through this area and drained into the river near the Upper Landing.

A waterfall tumbled over a limestone ledge at Tenth and Cedar streets; the stream drained into a lake at Eighth and Robert, then ran down to the Mississippi through a ravine between Jackson and Sibley. A hill bounded by present-day Jackson and Wall, and Fourth and Eighth streets was known variously as Baptist Hill (for the church built there), Mount Pisgah, and Burbank's Hill. In the 1870s the streets were cut through along the four sides of Smith (now Mears) Park, leaving the park sitting on a plateau about fifty feet high. At the Lower Landing, a bog extending from Sibley Street to Dayton's Bluff filled the area between Fourth Street and the river.

The first settlers built rough-hewn cabins of crossed logs, with doors and windows cut into the logs. Cracks were plastered with clay and marsh hay. Tables and benches were made of split logs and a one-legged bedstead was fitted into a corner of the cabin. Supplies had to be shipped in, and the women pieced out the pork, flour, tea, and sugar with wild rice, cranberries, honey, and maple sugar.

Life was not dull. When Vetal Guerin and Adele Perry were married in 1841, guests danced all night to Denis Cherrier's violin. Some days later, Guerin was leaning on his gatepost when a number of Indians, having passed several hours at Parrant's saloon, fired at him, the ball striking the post. Again, one morning Guerin opened his front door and an iron-headed arrow whizzed past him, striking the door jamb. Theirs was an eventful honeymoon.

The first business of the community was survival, and in 1842 Henry Jackson arrived to open the town's first store, the most important event since Father Galtier built his chapel. Jackson sold general merchandise and "liquid" goods and served as justice of the peace. Four years later he became the first postmaster. The post office was a two-foot-square candlebox he set up in his store. Customers helped themselves.

A man named Gerou opened the first meat market, and William Dugas bought 160 acres on Phalen Creek and built a grist and saw mill, the first industries in St. Paul. John R. Irvine arrived in 1843, bought 300 acres from Joseph Rondo, moved onto Rondo's old cabin near the present Civic Center, and logged off the timber covering most of Upper Town. He operated a sawmill and sold the wood to steamboat captains.

Irvine, William E. Hartshorn, Auguste L. Larpenteur, and Louis Robert arrived about the same time. Robert had been a fur trader in St. Louis. When he arrived in 1844, St. Paul had five stores, all of which sold whiskey; one tavern; one chapel; and twenty or so log dwellings. In 1846 Robert built the first frame building of hand-hewn lumber. He bought Parrant's claim and part of Gervais' and entered into the Indian trade.

Hartshorn also established a trading post. The first Ramsey County deed, dated April 23, 1844, records Hartshorn's purchase from Jackson, for $1,000, of "half of three acres, it being the place where said Jackson now lives, lying immediately on the Mississippi River, known as the Saint Paul's Landing."

Larpenteur lived to be the last survivor of the early men of influence and substance who built St. Paul. Their livelihood, and the livelihood of the settlers who followed them, hinged importantly on river transportation. In 1847 Henry Sibley, Henry M. Rice, and Hercules L. Dousman, who lived at Prairie du Chien, organized the Galena Packet Company to run regular packets from Galena, Illinois, to St. Paul. Their boat, the *Argo*, sank near the end of her first season, but she had

B

A *The* Pioneer and Democrat *office as it looked between 1854 and 1859 when it stood on the southeast corner of Third and Jackson. John S. Prince later moved the building to Eighth Street.*
B *Robert Street in 1851. Log house on right is on northwest corner of Third and Robert. In the distance is First Baptist Church on Baptist Hill, now Mears Park.*

A

B

C

A   John Irvine's house at Third and Franklin, about
     where the Minnesota Club is today. Irvine's claim of
     land embraced most of Uppertown.
B   Moffett's Temperance House, 1852, at the corner of
     Fourth and Jackson. The Jackson Street bridge
     crosses the old ravine that ran through the area.
C   St. Paul's first hardware store, established in 1849
     by John McCloud at Third and Cedar.
D   Vetal Guerin's house in 1852. This story-and-a-half
     house, built after the French fashion, stood at
     Seventh and Wabasha.

D

launched the river transportation system that kept St. Paul alive during its first two decades and has helped sustain the region since that time.

St. Paul, as the fur-trading center of the Northwest, was the collecting depot for furs coming in from the West and North, the supply center for traders heading back to their posts, and the place where furs were unloaded and transferred to warehouses for shipment down the river to railroad terminals, and to the East and Europe. The fur trade was dependent upon the steamboats that called at the Lower and Upper Landings, but overland travel and shipping were increasingly important to the survival of the trade. In 1844 the first Red River ox carts arrived in St. Paul, brought south from Pembina by Norman W. Kittson, then a trader on the Red River for the Hudson's Bay Company, and for the next two decades the arrival of the carts in St. Paul was one of the most colorful events of the summer.

Cumbersome and lumbering, the carts were made entirely of wood and could carry as much as 800 pounds of freight. They had six-to-seven-foot spoked wheels held together with wooden pegs and rawhide made from buffalo skins. The carts were pulled by oxen. Trudging along just ahead of the carts were their drivers, the *bois brulés*, who wore coarse blue cloth with brass buttons, red sashes, beaded caps, and Indian moccasins.

Caravans left the Red River early in June and were in St. Paul by early July, their arrival signaled hours before they appeared by the incessant screech of the unlubricated wheels. The first train brought in by Kittson consisted of six carts. It carried $1,400 in pelts, and left some $12,000 with St. Paul merchants for supplies hauled back to the Red River country. Within twenty years, ox-cart trains would be bringing into St. Paul annually more than $250,000 in raw pelts, pemmican, buffalo robes, foodstuffs, and other goods. Profits on the furs, combined with the money spent on supplies, represented more than a million dollars in income for the merchants. In 1851, 102 carts made the long journey to St. Paul, in 1857, 500, and in 1858, 600.

The first school teachers arrived. In 1845 Mrs. Matilda Rumsey established a small school in a log building near the Upper Landing where she taught for a few months. Harriet E. Bishop, however, is considered St. Paul's first permanent schoolteacher. She arrived in Minnesota from Vermont in 1847, organized a Sunday School, and taught a day school for a year. An interpreter was needed for those pupils who spoke only French or Sioux. School met in a log cabin on the corner of Third and St. Peter streets, its seats rough boards placed on pegs driven into the log walls.

Harriet Bishop was a remarkable woman. She once described herself, with a typically Victorian flourish, as a "feeble and timid young lady," but she apparently was neither. According to T.M. Newson, an early St. Paul editor, she was "angular, positive, determined — such a woman as is necessary for frontier life . . . tall, with a good figure; a bright, expressive face; earnest and decided in manners, and quick in speech."

Other amenities of civilization were introduced. Jacob W. Bass built the first hotel, the St. Paul House, out of tamarack logs, and the first ladies' sewing society, the "Circle of Industry," was organized to raise money for a new schoolhouse.

In 1847 the town site of some ninety acres was surveyed by Benjamin and Ira Brunson. There was not much, however, in the way of town government. From 1840 to 1849, St. Paul was part of St. Croix County, Territory of Wisconsin, and the county seat was at Stillwater. Except for the justices of the peace — Joseph R. Brown on Grey Cloud Island, Henry Sibley at Mendota, and Henry Jackson at St. Paul — much of the governing force in the St. Paul area was vested in the churches as the earliest organizations in the community. The Catholics' little log chapel, built by Father Galtier, became the first cathedral of a newly-formed diocese. The Methodists began holding services in Jackson's store in 1844, and in 1849 they built St. Paul's first Protestant church, the First Methodist Church. The Baptists and the Presbyterians arrived that year, and founded the First Baptist Church, now at Ninth and Wacouta streets, and the First Presbyterian Church, now House of Hope, whose first building stood near the site of the St. Paul Public Library.

On March 3, 1849, Minnesota became a territory, with St. Paul as its capital. News of the event did not reach the settlement until April 9, 1849, when the first steamboat of the season, the *Dr. Franklin No. 2*, rounded the bend at Dayton's Bluff in the midst of a thunderstorm, and put in at the Lower Landing.

The effect on St. Paul was immediate and profound. In the next three weeks, the village doubled in size. Seventy new buildings were erected, bringing to 142 the total number of buildings in the town.

One of the first acts of the new territorial governor, Alexander Ramsey, was to order a census of the territory. It listed 4,535 people in Minnesota; 910 in St. Paul; 609 in Stillwater; 248 in St. Anthony; and 322 in Little Canada (founded by Benjamin Gervais and other French families who had moved out from St. Paul in 1844).

In his 1876 *History of St. Paul and Ramsey County*, J. Fletcher Williams published a remarkable list of residents of St. Paul in 1850. The list included only men and it reflected the strongly

A *Four of Louis Robert's small fleet of steamboats tied up at the Lower Landing in 1859.*
B *Governor Alexander Ramsey, about 1844. From a daguerreotype owned by his granddaughters, Laura and Anna Furness.*
C *Harriet E. Bishop.*
D *Red River ox carts lined up in 1859 in front of Cheritree and Farwell on Third Street.*

A

B

C

14

D

. eggs at nineteen cents a dozen; butter at twenty cents a pound . . .

French character of the town. The Canadian French and Swiss settlers made up the major portion of the population, and the ability to speak French was indispensable to the traders of that time.

On April 27, 1849, the first newspaper printed in the territory, the *Minnesota Pioneer*, was issued by James M. Goodhue. Before the end of the year, D.A. Robertson had established the *Minnesota Democrat*. J.P. Owens followed with *The Minnesotian*, and T.M. Newson with the *Times*. Joseph R. Brown took over the *Pioneer* after Goodhue's death. Readers were treated to a lively and highly individualistic account of life in St. Paul. These early editors often were ardently prideful where Minnesota was concerned, frequently the foremost boosters of settlement, and, in their personal style, untrammeled examples of the colorful era of personal journalism. Their like will not be seen again.

The first editions of the *Pioneer* reflect something of the way of life for the early settlers of St. Paul. Corn sold at fifty cents a bushel; eggs at nineteen cents a dozen; butter at twenty cents a pound; coffee

was ten cents a pound; fresh beef, $9 per hundred pounds; and a bottle of whiskey — "market well supplied, sales dull at 25 cents." Some 2,000 bushels of cranberries were shipped out during the 1849 season; the first stage line between St. Paul and St. Anthony began operation, and D.F. Brawley burned the first bricks made in Minnesota in a brick yard near Summit between Dayton and Marshall avenues.

The first business directory, issued by the *Pioneer* on January 1, 1850, included five clergymen, fourteen lawyers, two land agents, four doctors, sixteen mercantile firms, one shoemaker, six hotels, three painters, two blacksmiths, four plasterers, five masons, eighteen carpenters, one silversmith, one gunsmith, five bakers, three wheelwrights, one harnessmaker, and one tinner.

And on September 12, 1851, William Taylor, barber and hair dresser, announced in *The Minnesotian* that he had "built and fitted up a Shaving Saloon, on 3rd street, next door west of the new Post Office in Saint Paul, up to the increasing luxury, style and elegance of the growing metropolis of Minnesota, where he will be happy to serve citizens and strangers in St. Paul, in every branch of his business, according to the best of his ability."

Ramsey County was one of nine counties created with the organization of the territory; its western boundary extended northwest along the Mississippi to Elk River, then north to Deerwood, beyond Mille Lacs, and south, again to the Mississippi River, which formed the southern boundary. Dr. David Day was elected register of deeds; C.V.P. Bull, sheriff; J.W. Simpson, treasurer; Louis Robert, Benjamin Gervais, and R.P. Russell, commissioners; and Henry A. Lambert, judge of probate.

Before the end of 1849, the 233-mile military road, the Point Douglas Road, had been completed, linking St. Paul with Prairie du Chien. St. Paul's residents could look forward to the time when they no longer would be isolated during the winter. St. Paul's emergence from primitive simplicity was beginning. Among the new articles of luxury prepared in St. Paul was ice cream, available from a Mr. Bates, a baker on Third Street. The *Pioneer* described another landmark in this inexorable march toward civilization:

"Within the present week, the citizens of St. Paul have erected on the lower square a pump. Of course, nothing could be more desirable or to the city more appropriate, for what is a town without a pump? A town pump is useful on many occasions. It is the center of exchange, where merchants and financiers do the fiats of commerce. It is the place for placards of advertisement. A reference for details of information upon all doubtful questions. As we say, 'Inquire of the town pump.' It might be the stand for a temperance lecturer. It might answer as a whipping post for rogues of low degree; and might subserve a patriotic purpose as a ducking engine with which to quench the heat of overzealous office seekers."

It is little wonder that 1850 dawned auspiciously. The gentlemen of the city inaugurated the practice of "making calls" on New Year's Day, an important social function for many years. A ball, with about 100 couples attending, was held at the Central House, the first of several such social occasions that winter. In the *Pioneer*, Goodhue helpfully advised gentlemen not to wear pumps, moccasins or heavy boots and declared that, "it is ill-bred, yes! and ill gotten bread, for a lady to sweep a quantity of cakes and nuts into her handkerchief, at the table, to carry home. She might as well pocket the sugar bowl and the tea-spoons."

From 1850 to 1858, the rush of immigrants into St. Paul was heavy, spurred by the 1851 Treaty of Traverse des Sioux which opened to settlement the lands drained by the Minnesota River. The number of steamboats docking at St. Paul rose steadily: forty-one in 1844, forty-six in 1847, sixty-three in 1848, ninety-five in 1849, 1,068 in 1858. In May, 1857, twenty-four boats were tied up at the Lower Landing in a single day.

According to Williams, an estimated 30,000 immigrants arrived in Minnesota in 1855. He points to 1855, 1856, and 1857 as "the three great years of immigration in our Territorial days." The population of the territory leaped to 53,000 in 1855; Ramsey County had 9,475 residents, and St. Paul, 4,716.

Hotels and boarding houses were so crowded that people camped in the streets. Amelia Ullman, the wife of Joseph Ullman, an early St. Paul merchant, left a vivid account of that period which was published in the Autumn, 1954, issue of the Minnesota Historical Society's quarterly magazine, *Minnesota History*. She wrote: "Near what was then the end of Third Street we stopped before a long, white, frame building the long side towards Third Street and with an 'L' at each end of the rear. This . . . was the American House, one of the principal hotels . . . . The only room that the proprietor could

place at our disposal was the little one that my husband had been occupying but had found too small for his own convenience . . . .

"Life in the little stuffy room under the hot sun became so miserable that one evening I rushed out of the hotel and went myself to the row of shanties near by enquiring if any of the occupants could direct me to a house that was to be rented . . . .One crumbling old shanty with a flight of crazy steps leading up to the front door . . .was pointed out as the only house to be rented in St. Paul. Late one evening in August a man whom we had commissioned to get a house for us, came excitedly into the hotel and said that if my husband would accompany him immediately he might be able to secure a house.

"In a few days we moved into the second story of a white frame house in the rear of the American House. Only a conscientious housewife, only a devoted mother who had lived in St. Paul in those days knows all the inconveniences and miseries that I was forced to endure in my efforts to do what I felt to be my duty. No servants, no house help of any kind was to be obtained. Every drop of water used

Life in the little stuffy room under the hot sun became so miserable that one evening...

A *Emigration into Minnesota boosted by broadsides. This extols the virtues of Nininger, near Hastings.*
B *The American House, shown in 1858, at Third and Exchange streets. Originally the Rice House, it was destroyed by fire in 1863.*

B

had to be carried across the prairie from a well in a livery stable back of the American House; and to get this it was necessary to crowd in among drivers and rough men from the prairies.

"My child was ill much of the time from lack of proper nourishment, for good wholesome food was difficult to obtain. Fresh vegetables and fruit were unknown. These things being brought up from St. Louis by the boats, they were often in such a condition upon their arrival at St. Paul that their use would have been deleterious to health."

Mrs. Ullman finally was directed to the St. Paul Market House "across the prairie at some distance from my home" (at Seventh and Wabasha). She found it almost empty. Then, "As I came out of the building I met a woman carrying some butter and cheese; and, when I found that she had these for sale, I greeted her as if she were an old friend. The woman said that she was the owner of the only cow in town and agreed to furnish me weekly with milk and butter . . . ."

Land speculation spread through the community in the first of Minnesota's great real estate booms. In 1854 Henry McKenty, the most successful of the speculators at that time, bought several thousand acres of prairie land in Washington County for $1.25 per acre. The next year he sold it for $5 an acre. At the same time, he was offering 42 per cent interest per year for working capital.

One of the 1856 arrivals was a young man from a small farm near Toronto, Canada. James J. Hill went to work as a clerk for the Dubuque and St. Paul Packet Company. Another pioneer in the transportation business, James Crawford Burbank, had arrived in 1851 and formed the Northwestern Express Company, a stagecoach line that spread into a network of 1,600 miles of overland routes throughout the territory. Hill and his associate, Norman W. Kittson, built their railroad system on the foundations of Burbank's empire.

St. Paul was a community struggling to organize itself. The town was incorporated in 1854 and David Olmsted was elected mayor; W.R. Miller, city marshal; D.L. Fuller, treasurer; James Starkey, police justice; and George L. Becker, president of the city council.

It was still a frontier town, with a fragile veneer of civilization. The Sons of Temperance — that universal response to the inevitable problem of liquor — pressured the legislature into passing a stiff law forbidding the manufacture, sale, or possession of liquor, prohibiting liquor dealers from sitting as jurymen, and requiring destruction of all liquor in the territory. However, the act was written to self-destruct, depending upon the voters' willingness to allow morality to be legislated. Ramsey County's free spirits did not take kindly to such wholesale invasion of their rights and enforcement was erratic, not to say non-existent. When the sheriff confiscated some liquor a merchant named William Constans had stored in his warehouse, Constans and his friends resisted. A crowd gathered, and the excitement almost led to a riot. Without much delay, the supreme court of the territory declared the law null and void.

Then there was the "duel" — a brawl, actually — between James M. Goodhue and Joseph Cooper. On January 14, 1854, Goodhue published a venomous denunciation of Cooper's brother, Judge David Cooper, a bitter political enemy. Goodhue accused the judge of drunkenness, lechery, and playing cards on Sunday. The next day Joseph Cooper attacked Goodhue in the street. Both had pistols, which the sheriff promptly confiscated, but Cooper then pulled out a knife and stabbed Goodhue in the abdomen. Goodhue broke away and shot Cooper with a second pistol he was carrying. Cooper again rushed at Goodhue and stabbed him in the back. The two men finally were separated. Both were seriously wounded. The incident caused much excitement, and

Goodhue and Joseph Cooper.

A

B

A *The state's first Capitol, the domed building on the left in this 1871 photograph of downtown St. Paul. Built in 1853 at Tenth and Wabasha, it was destroyed by fire in 1881. In 1883 a new Capitol was completed on the same site, and it remained standing for several decades after erection of the present Capitol.*

B *Judge David Cooper, Goodhue's political enemy.*

A

A *St. Paul Bridge, predecessor of the present Wabasha
   Street bridge, erected as a toll bridge in 1859 and
   replaced in 1874.*
B *A dog train just in from Fort Gerry in 1859 at Walnut
   Street and Pleasant Avenue. Summit Avenue was
   lined even at this early date with homes. The square
   house with the cupola, at left, is the David Stuart
   house and it is still standing at 312 Summit. The
   small building just behind the drivers is the first
   House of Hope Presbyterian Church.*
C *Red Coach Line owned by Alvaren Allen and C.L.
   Chase in 1856.*

B

RED COACH LINE.

ALLEN & CHASE, PROPRIETORS.

OFFICE NEXT DOOR BELOW THE AMERICAN HOUSE.

Leave St. Paul Daily for Anoka, Monticello, St. Cloud, Sauk Rapids, Little Falls,
Ripley, and Crow Wing.

STAGES FOR ST ANTHONY AND MINNEAPOLIS ARE AT THE LEVEE, AT ALL TIMES, ON THE ARRIVAL OF BOATS.

C

a public meeting was held for ''all the lovers of decency . . . who feel any interest in the reputation of our Territory.'' Lawlessness was deplored, and soothing resolutions were passed, which restored public tranquillity. Cooper and Goodhue both survived the duel, but Goodhue died suddenly a few months later, possibly of cholera.

Next came the shoot-out at the ''Minnesota Outfit'' in the heart of St. Paul. Eighteen Chippewa ambushed a number of Sioux in revenge for the killing of a Chippewa. The Sioux had just entered the American Fur Company's trading house at Jackson and Third streets when the Chippewas rushed up, fired into the store, fatally wounded one of the Sioux, a woman, and fled. A platoon of dragoons was called out from Fort Snelling to pursue them. They caught up with the Indians near St. Croix Falls, Wisconsin, fired on them and killed one of them. The others escaped.

The first Capitol was completed in 1853 at Tenth and Cedar; the first county courthouse built at Fourth and Wabasha in 1852; the first city hall erected on the present site of the Old Federal Courts Building; a ferry opened to the west side of the Mississippi; the second Cathedral of St. Paul constructed at Sixth and St. Peter in 1851; and work begun on the first bridge across the river. The predecessor of the present Wabasha Street bridge, it was known simply as the St. Paul bridge, and it was a toll bridge until 1874 — five cents for foot passengers, twenty-five cents for two-horse teams.

Newspaper editors had been calling for a jail for some time: '' We need a jail far more than we do a court-house,'' observed *The Minnesotian.* ''The criminal law is almost a dead letter for want of a jail to lock up rogues in . . . .'' '' Fights on Sunday are becoming entirely too frequent an occurrence,'' another editor complained, ''and it behooves every good citizen to lend a helping hand to our efficient marshal in preserving the quiet of the city.'' And so

21

the first Ramsey County jail — the first prison in Minnesota — was built behind the courthouse. A small log building covered with boards, it was replaced by a stone structure in 1857.

A far more serious matter was the mysterious death of Stanislaus Bilanski, who had settled in St. Paul in 1842. Bilanski had a talent for marrying and divorcing women. In 1859 his fourth wife apparently poisoned him, or so it was decided by the jury that tried and convicted her of murder. On March 23, 1859, Annie Bilanski was hanged in the presence of an immense crowd, the first white person executed for murder in Minnesota.

Other institutions were founded during the 1850s. Oakland Cemetery was organized in 1853 after *The Minnesotian* declared that, "It is an utter disgrace to St. Paul, that with all her spirit of improvement and public enterprise, we have no place to bury the dead. The tract of land now used for a burial place is private property, and liable to be sold for other

purposes at any moment . . . . Who will be the first to call a meeting for the formation of a Cemetery Association?" St. Joseph's Hospital also was founded in 1853. The Pioneer Guard, the state's first volunteer military organization, was formed in 1856 and it was much in demand for such civic and social events as parades, Fourth of July celebrations, the laying of the numerous cornerstones required in the growing town, and military balls, all a very real part of the community's social life.

"The ball this evening at the Winslow House promises to be a splendid affair," the *Pioneer* declared on July 4, 1856. "The Pioneer Guard have received the most beautiful uniforms throughout, and the members will appear on this occasion in full parade dress . . ." The Sixth Regiment Band from Fort Snelling provided the music for many of these balls, as well as for steamboat excursions, another popular diversion.

There were other amusements. On June 21, 1856,

A

the H.H. Smith American Circus exhibited in Rice Park, the public square deeded to the city by Henry M. Rice in 1849, the same year Irvine Park and Smith Park were given to the city.

These early parks were simply untended open spaces at first. For awhile, Rice Park was occupied by a German florist who was allowed to cultivate flowers and vegetables in return for caring for the park. Then a fence was erected, but the square continued to look forlorn, so the mayor procured some trees. The chief of police and his men planted them but, because of the underlying rock formation, people were skeptical about their survival. *The Minnesotian* commented: "It is a fact, ascertained by actual observation, that at least one, if not two, of the shade trees in the City park are alive."

Cows were a problem. They kept wandering into the park until spikes were installed on the turnstiles. There was another difficulty. The neighborhood women were in the habit of beating their rugs in the park. A law was passed prohibiting this, but the practice continued until a police officer, in a fit of exasperation, finally ordered them out: "The mayor has said stop, the chief has said stop, and now I say unto you stop!"

Smith Park, named for an Illinois real estate speculator who never lived in St. Paul, had no such problems, with its fifty-foot plateau. The hill was gradually reduced as the dirt was hauled away to fill bogs and ravines, but as late as 1912 the park was strewn with large glacial boulders. Irvine Park, as the center of a fashionable residential district, was the most elegant of the three parks.

By the summer of 1857, St. Paul, with a population of almost 10,000, was supporting three professional theatrical companies, a minstrel show, a circus, a professional tent show, and an amateur dramatic society. Seven players from Placide's Varieties in New Orleans had opened a two-week engagement at

B

A *The* War Eagle, *built in 1854, the second of five steamboats by that name. This was the boat that carried the First Minnesota Infantry Regiment off to the Civil War. It burned in 1870.*

B *Broadside printed in April, 1858, by the* Pioneer and Democrat.

Settlers brought along the comforts of civilization . . .

A

B

C

D

E

F

G

A *Quilting frame, dating from about 1760. The quilt is a variation of the log cabin pattern called "California Trail." Quilts, the most versatile of pioneer coverings, were pieced together from scraps of material saved from dresses, curtains, suits, and blankets. Family members and neighbors worked together on "quilting bees," finishing quilts in one day and exchanging news of the community.*

B *China Doll, about 1860, prized possession of many frontier children. To save room in their trunks, families often brought just the china head as they moved West, and made the bodies later from rags or straw covered with scraps of material.*

C *Simple, sturdy, white ironware dishes, dating from 1860, on a bright, hand woven tablecloth. As they prospered, settlers acquired more elaborate china, and kerosene lamps replaced the foul-smelling tallow candles.*

D *Wood-burning range, about 1850. Factory-made and indispensable for early homes, the wood-burning range quickly displaced the fireplace for St. Paul housewives who could easily purchase them. A wood-burning range was a status symbol throughout the Midwest.*

E *An 1850s butter mold, with the pineapple motif that graced many such molds. The mold rests on a tin grater, hand-punched with a square nail.*

F *Corner shelf with 1850 utensils. Household utensils often hung above a dry sink which, with a wooden pail of water, was the standard "dish-washer" of the time. On the shelf, left to right, are a molded candle, an egg basket, a basting brush made from a turkey wing, a hand-carved mortar and pestle, a tin candle mold, a coffee grinder, and a bean pot. Below the shelf are a hand-carved potato masher, ladle, copper strainer, tin sifter, dipped tallow and beeswax candles, the family mirror, and a salt container.*

G *Pantry or cupboard, about 1850. Few kitchens could do without a pantry to hold the family's china, cooking utensils, and foodstuffs. Handmade from rough-hewed wood, such examples of pioneer workmanship are prized today as "primitives." (Photographed at the Ramsey County Historical Society's Gibbs Farm Museum.)*

A

Mazurka Hall, Third Street and Exchange, on August 12, 1851. It was the first professional theater performance in the territory.

On the last night of their engagement, the house was "crowded to suffocation," according to the *Pioneer.* This was an apt description. In a letter written about 1852, Sara Fuller described another performance:

"There was no windows, excepting in front, and the staging took those off, and all the air there was for the audience were the skylights overhead. We had been there about ten minutes when it commenced raining and they closed the skylights, and it was an oppressive warm night and they had been closed about five minutes when I began to grow faint and Sam went out with me to the door, and went for a tumbler of water for me and when he came back I had fainted and fell upon the doorstep . . . . My bonnet was completely covered with mud, I was lamed on one side of my face and had to wear a patch for more than a week. I did not attend any more theatre parties."

The glamorous Sally St. Clair brought "The St. Louis Varieties" to St. Paul for several seasons and captivated the men, but the city's theatrical fixture was the People's Theatre built by Henry Van Liew.

B

C

It was a temporary structure with wooden benches, but it had a capable company of seasoned performers. Van Liew wanted to give St. Paul a permanent year-round theater but the financial panic of 1857 made it difficult to keep the doors open. In 1859, fire destroyed the theater and Van Liew left St. Paul.

The German Reading Society was incorporated in 1854, and in 1858 the Society built the Atheneum, a one-story frame structure on the corner of Walnut and Exchange streets that became a popular gathering place for the Germans of St. Paul. Music was flourishing, and the German Singing Society was formed in 1853. Other singing groups were the Liederkranz Society, the Beethoven Society, and the Arlan Society.

Professor Phillip Rohr arrived in 1858 from Philadelphia, where he had been conductor of the Handel and Haydn Societies, and soon was energetically organizing concerts and operas. In 1859 he presented two contemporary operas, ''Il Trovatore,'' then only six years old, and '' Daughter of the Regiment,'' which had its premiere in Europe in 1840.

In 1857 William Markoe made the first balloon ascension in Minnesota from the site of today's

27

The disunion cloud was darkening the southe

State Capitol. A pioneer in aeronautics, Markoe made his flight in a craft measuring 136 feet around and fifty feet in height. He reached an altitude of three miles and covered forty-five miles in an hour and a half.

The first *St. Paul City Directory*, issued in 1857, listed some 1,700 names, along with advertisements for 158 business establishments. This was a year of wild and extravagant land speculation, not only in St. Paul but throughout the country. The bubble burst in August when the failure of the Ohio Life Insurance and Trust Company of New York precipitated the nation-wide Panic of 1857. In St. Paul, the bank owned by Charles W.W. Borup and Charles Oakes suspended payment for about ten days. Four more banks closed their doors. Only three banks, Parker Paine, Mackubin and Edgerton, and Willius Brothers, remained in business. The supply of money dried up, new construction slid to a halt, and mortgages were foreclosed. The city's population dropped almost 50 per cent in a month as settlers who had arrived in the hope of making fortunes retreated to the East.

The city and county were authorized to issue paper money as a medium of exchange, and the city's merchants held a series of meetings to try to work out some means of relief. A barter system took over.

"There is one thing on which we can congratulate ourselves this winter," the *St. Paul Advertiser* observed in October of 1857. ". . . even if the utter paralysis of business intercourse between the East and the West should lock up our abundant harvest in our own teeming granaries, we will at least have enough to eat, and won't have to pay six or seven dollars a week for board."

"Retrenchment is the order of the day, because it is an absolute necessity of the day," the *Advertiser's* editor advised his readers. "One half of the expenses of nine-tenths of the men, women, and children, in our towns especially, are for needless luxuries. We do not blame anyone in ordinary times for enjoying themselves . . . . But the expensive gratifications of fast horses, fast women & [company] are not of a class exactly which an honorable man will pursue beyond his means . . . ." And the *Pioneer and Democrat* reported that, "The laboring men on the Levee contract struck yesterday for ten hours time and increased wages. During the winter this work has been the last resort of them who were obliged to work or starve, and the consequence was, wages were reduced to the lowest point possible, to provide food enough to keep the body in a fit condition for work. The laborers demand $1 per day for ten hours. We presume there will be no hesitation about giving the wages asked."

In 1857, to the dismay of St. Paul's residents, a bill to move the capital to St. Peter passed the territorial legislature and was on its way to enrollment and signature by the governor when Joe Rolette, chairman of the enrollment committee, intervened.

Contrary to the stories which have arisen about him, Rolette was an educated and intelligent

French-Canadian, and the son of an important fur trader at Prairie du Chien. A colorful man who wore Indian garb at home, he was the legislative representative from Pembina, now in northeastern North Dakota. Rolette was sympathetic to St. Paul's cause, but he also may have been motivated simply by his well-known sense of humor.

At any rate, when the bill reached him, he tucked it in his pocket, walked over to Truman and Smith's bank and locked it in the vault. Then he had his room changed at the Fuller House and "disappeared." During the next five days, as the legislature met in continuous session for 123 hours, Rolette hid out, his friends gravely reporting him somewhere in the vicinity of Sauk Rapids and heading north on his dog sled.

At noon on March 7, as the legislature's time expired, Rolette reappeared with the bill. Legal opinion subsequently held that no law had been passed, and St. Paul remained the capital.

During the winter of 1857, a constitutional convention was held in St. Paul in preparation for statehood, and Minnesota's individualistic politics surfaced. The convention immediately split down party lines. Republican and Democratic factions, meeting separately for a month, drafted two separate constitutions. It was obvious, even to those involved, that the only way to avoid national ridicule, to say nothing of legal challenges, was to combine the two constitutions. On August 27, 1857, a conference committee did so. The next day, both conventions adopted the constitution. It was

ratified on October 13, 1857, and on May 11, 1858, Minnesota was admitted to the Union as its thirty-second state.

The word reached St. Paul on May 14. There were no demonstrations. Henry Hastings Sibley was quietly sworn in as governor; J.M. Cavanaugh and W.W. Phelps prepared to leave for Washington as the state's first representatives, and Henry M. Rice and General James Shields as its senators.

In the fall of 1859, grain was exported from Minnesota for the first time, and people began to sniff prosperity in the air again. But 1860 closed under gloomy circumstances, Williams reported. "The disunion cloud was darkening the southern horizon," he wrote, "and the mutterings of war were heard in the distance."

... were heard in the distance.

Washington City
April 14, 1861

Hon. Simon Cameron
    Secy War
            Sir

            As the Executive of
the State of Minnesota I hereby tender
to the Government of the U States, on the
part of that state one thousand men,
to be ready for service so soon as
the necessary information can be com=
municated to the people there.

            As the Legislature is not in session
and will not be unless specially con=
vened before January of next year,
May I ask whether you would feel
justified in saying that the reasonable
expenses that may be incurred will be
furnished by the General Governt, in view
of the facts above stated

            I am pleased to say that in all
this I have the advice and support of
the Senators from Minnesota and know
that it will be heartily and promptly
responded to this action

                    Very respectfully
                    Your obt. svt.
                        Alex. Ramsey

Part Two/A Mighty Empire Will Emerge

In April, 1861, Alexander Ramsey, who succeeded Henry H. Sibley as governor of Minnesota, was in Washington, D.C. He later recalled the day the Civil War began:

"The knots of earnest men . . . in the corridors and reading rooms of the hotels indicated . . that there was an impending peril. On Saturday night, April 13th, the population of Washington was deeply moved by the intelligence that Fort Sumter . . . had been attacked . . . and that the garrison had surrendered. Early Sunday morning . . . I visited the war department and found Secretary [of War Simon P.] Cameron . . . about to leave his office.

"I said, 'My business is simply as governor of Minnesota to tender a thousand men to defend the government.'

" 'Sit down immediately,' he replied, 'and write the tender you have made, as I am now on my way to the President's mansion.'

"This was quickly done and thus Minnesota became the first to cheer President Lincoln by offers of assistance in the crisis which had arrived."

Lincoln immediately called for 75,000 militia to serve for three months and Cameron notified Ramsey that Minnesota's quota would be one regiment of 780 men. Ramsey telegraphed instructions to Lieutenant Governor Ignatius Donnelly to issue the first call for volunteers.

Tradition has designated Josias King of St. Paul's Pioneer Guard as the first man to volunteer for service in the First Minnesota Infantry. In 1903 a bronze statue of King, who settled down in St. Paul after the war, was erected in Summit Park, and it stands today on John Ireland Boulevard, down the hill from the Cathedral.

King enlisted in Company A, organized by Alexander Wilkin from among his fellow Pioneer Guard members. Wilkin, a captain in the Mexican

---

Alexander Ramsey's letter offering Minnesota troops to the Union after the fall of Fort Sumter.

*... Minnesota became the first ... by offers of
assistance in the crisis ...*

War, had moved to St. Paul in 1849, practiced law, and served as secretary of the territory.

While Wilkin organized Company A, William H. Acker resigned as adjutant general of Minnesota and organized the St. Paul Volunteers into Company C. Seven more companies were added, to complete the First Infantry's roster. Most of the officers were St. Paul men. Willis A. Gorman, a former territorial governor, was colonel; Dr. J.H. Stewart, surgeon; and the Reverend E.D. Neill, chaplain. On May 1, 1861, the regiment was mustered into federal service at Fort Snelling.

Clothing for the troops was a problem. Adjutant General John B. Sanborn promptly solved it by placing an order with Culver and Farrington, a St.

Paul dry goods and clothing store. The firm's bill listed:

868 blankets for men, at $3	$2,604.00
13 blankets for hospital, at $3	39.00
800 flannel shirts, at $1.50	1,200.00
975 pairs wool socks, at 25¢	243.75
868 hats, at $2.25	1,953.00
868 pairs pants, at $4.50	3,906.00
868 pairs drawers, at 62-1/2¢	542.50
	$10,488.25

The uniforms were picturesque — red flannel shirts, black pantaloons, and black felt slouch hats. On June 22 the regiment started from Fort Snelling for the East aboard the *Northern Belle* and the *War Eagle.* The steamboats put the men ashore at the

*Josias King, nominated by tradition as the first
man to volunteer for service in the First Minnesota
Infantry Regiment.*

A

A   *Officers of the First Minnesota Infantry Regiment at Fort Snelling in 1861.*

B&C   *Members of the First Minnesota Infantry Regiment after the Battle of Fair Oaks in 1862.*

B

C

Upper Landing for a parade through town, and the *Pioneer* reported:

"They marched up Eagle Street to Third, down Third to Jackson, and down Jackson to the lower levee where they embarked. A vast crowd assembled at the levee to see them off. There were some affecting scenes of leave-taking, but the soldiers stood it bravely. The line of boats cast off at half past 8 o'clock, the band playing a lively air, the crowd on the shore and the soldiers cheering lustily." Two ladies accompanied the regiment — the wives of Major William H. Dyke and

Adjutant William B. Leach.

The regiment was the first of twenty-one units recruited in Minnesota during the war years and it is the most famous because of its spectacular charge during the Battle of Gettysburg fought on July 1-3, 1863. Colonel William Colvill of Red Wing was in command of the First Minnesota and, after marching steadily north from Virginia, the regiment arrived on the battlefield on July 2. Three companies were detached for duty elsewhere, and the remaining 262 men were stationed in support of an artillery battery on Cemetery Ridge.

General Sickles' Third Corps was struggling with Confederate forces at the Peach Orchard. Near sunset, Sickles' lines gave way. His men poured past the First Minnesota's position to reform in the rear. Sickles had been wounded and General Winfield Scott Hancock was suddenly in command of the Third Corps. Hancock sent for reinforcements, but in minutes the Confederates would break through the lines. Desperately, Hancock turned toward the little band of Minnesota men.

"There was no organized force near to oppose them except our handful of 262 men," wrote William Lochren in *Minnesota in the Civil War and the Indian Wars.*

"Just then Hancock, with a single aide, rode up at full speed . . . calling out as he reached us, 'What regiment is this?'

"'First Minnesota,' replied Colvill.

"'Charge those lines,' commanded Hancock.

"Every man realized in an instant what that order meant . . . the sacrifice of the regiment to gain a few minutes' time . . ."

Moving at double time and not stopping to fire, the men neared the enemy's first line.

A *The charge of the First Minnesota at Gettysburg,
    from a panorama of the battle.*
B *Marshall Sherman, awarded the Congressional
    Medal of Honor for capturing the flag of the 28th
    Virginia Infantry Regiment during Pickett's charge
    at Gettysburg.*

"Charge," shouted Colvill, and with leveled
bayonets they rushed the enemy lines. The first line
broke and rushed back through the second line,
halting the entire advance. When the charge ended,
215 men of the First Regiment were dead or
wounded, the greatest percentage of loss suffered by
a Union regiment in one engagement during the
Civil War. Not a man was missing.
    Hancock wrote later:
    "I would have ordered that regiment in if I had
known that every man would be killed. It had to be
done, and I was glad to find such a gallant body of

Execution of thirty-eight Sioux at Mankato, a sad conclusion to the Sioux Uprising of 1862.

men at hand willing to make the terrible sacrifice that the occasion demanded."

The next day, the forty-seven* surviving men were stationed at the center of the Union line that repulsed Pickett's charge, regarded as the high point of the Confederacy. Seventeen more Minnesota men were killed or wounded, including all of the color guard. It was during Pickett's charge that Marshall Sherman of St. Paul plunged into the surging, struggling men, and emerged with the flag of the 28th Virginia Infantry Regiment. He was awarded the Congressional Medal of Honor, one of four Minnesotans, and the only man from St. Paul, to receive the medal during the Civil War.** Sherman later established the Sherman House at Fourth and Sibley streets, known as "the best two-dollar a day house in the country."

Out of St. Paul's 11,000 population at the beginning of the Civil War, 1,498 men — almost its entire voting population — served in the Union army and 124 of them died. Alexander Wilkin, who rose to the rank of general, was killed at the Battle of Tupelo, the highest ranking soldier from

Minnesota to lose his life. Captain William H. Acker was killed at Shiloh.

While the First Minnesota was being formed, the women of St. Paul organized the St. Paul Volunteer Aid Society, believed to be the first of its kind in the country. They scraped lint, sewed bandages, baked pies, and stirred up puddings. It was soon apparent that more durable contributions were needed. In six weeks the women made almost 900 emergency cases and twenty-five guard cases of oil cloth, bound with red tape. They supplied the men with needle books, towels, mosquito face nets, and they sewed 600 havelocks, a linen attachment for a cap that protected the neck from the sun.

"Eight ladies yesterday made fifty," reported the *Pioneer and Democrat* for June 18, 1861. "Ladies having sewing machines are called upon to lend a hand." They sewed in stifling heat in Ingersoll Hall, but gentlemen sent in refreshments, and a pail of iced lemonade from C.E. Mayo made an afternoon endurable.

Amelia Ullman recalled war-time St. Paul in an account now in the Minnesota Historical Society's documents collections:

"Recruiting stations were established at St. Paul," she wrote. "Patriotism became intense. Everywhere was there the sound of the fife and drum, the splendor of new uniforms and the burnishing of new arms. Homes were broken up by the departure of fathers and sons; the boat landing was almost daily the scene of sad partings."

Fourteen months after the first troops left for the South, the men who governed Minnesota from St.

---

*In tribute, this number is used as the designation for the 47th Division, Minnesota's National Guard.
**Three other St. Paul men were awarded Congressional Medals of Honor in later conflicts. They were Army Private John Tracy, for bravery in action at Chiricahua Mountain, Arizona, during the Indian Wars; Marine Corps Captain Jesse Farley Dyer, for distinguished conduct in the Battle of Vera Cruz, 1914; Richard E. Fleming, marine corps reserve, for heroism at the Battle of Midway, 1942. Fleming Field in South St. Paul is named for him.

Paul were suddenly faced with an ugly conflict little
more than 100 miles to the west — the Sioux
Uprising of August, 1862, led by Little Crow.

Sioux annuities due in late spring had been
delayed by a Congress distracted by the war in the
South, and the Sioux were hungry and desperate.
The gold was on its way from St. Paul when the
Indians began their attacks and it remained hidden
at Fort Ridgely when the fort was besieged on
August 20 and 23. Later the money was returned to
St. Paul.

After the Sioux Uprising ended September 23
with the Battle of Wood Lake, Little Crow and his
followers fled into the Dakotas where most of the
Sioux remaining in Minnesota eventually were
resettled. The sad story of how thirty-eight Sioux
were hanged at Mankato on December 26, 1862, is
well-known.

With the end of the Civil War, St. Paul shared in
the post-war prosperity that suffused the nation.

A

B

C

... a massive Victorian structure that cost $125,000.

The war had been costly, however; the city had spent $117,543 in the war effort and for relief for families of soldiers.

By 1865 St. Paul's population was 12,976, and the first railroad had been built, the harbinger of the extraordinary expansion that followed the war. The first rails in the state were laid in 1862 by the St. Paul and Pacific Railroad along the 10-mile stretch between St. Paul and St. Anthony. The road had been chartered in 1857 when Henry M. Rice, territorial delegate to Congress from Minnesota, secured a land grant of 4,500,000 acres for construction of six railroad lines. The Panic of 1857 put a halt to the work, but in 1862 the state contracted with Elias F. Drake and V. Winters to begin the road. Edmund Rice, the road's first president, was in England searching for capital and sent back 3,000 tons of rails. The first locomotive, named the "William Crooks" for its chief engineer, arrived in St. Paul by steamboat on September 9, 1861. The next spring, two small passenger cars arrived, again by steamboat. On June 28, 1862, the cars were coupled to the "William Crooks" and the first run made to St. Anthony.

During the next thirty years, the enormous transportation network created around the steam engine spread throughout the Northwest from its center at St. Paul. At one time at least twelve separate lines threaded in and out of the city, including the great trunk lines which connected St. Paul with Chicago. Among them were the Great Northern; the Northern Pacific; the Chicago, St. Paul, Minneapolis, and Omaha; the Minnesota Central; the Chicago Great Western; the Minneapolis and St. Louis; the Wisconsin Central; the Chicago, Rock Island and Pacific; the Minneapolis, St. Paul and Sault Ste. Marie (shortened to the familiar "Soo" line); the Chicago, Milwaukee, St. Paul, and Pacific; and the Chicago, Burlington and Quincy. The railroads helped to create the great fortunes associated with their leaders, but they also profoundly changed the lives of ordinary men and women living in St. Paul. This can be seen in the railroads' slogans: "Fast Mail Line to All Points in the Eastern United States and Canada"; "The Best Line to the Farming and Wheat Lands of Minnesota and Dakota"; "Only Line which Reaches Every Part of the Red River Valley"; "The Favorite Summer Excursion Route to Lake Superior and Eastern Points via the Great Lakes."

The rails carried the enormous numbers of immigrants who arrived in St. Paul from the East during this period. Thousands of them stayed, but others passed on through to settle the lands the railroads were opening up. They bought goods shipped out to them by St. Paul merchants, and sent their produce back to the Twin Cities for processing and shipping East.

Most of the lines serving St. Paul had headquarters there and provided jobs for an estimated one out of every four of the city's labor force. The first general office building of James J. Hill's Great Northern — a restrained, classical red brick structure — still stands at Kellogg Boulevard and Wall (Broadway) Street. The cast iron gate to the inner court where Hill stabled his horse can be seen on Wall. The Northern Pacific built a four-story Victorian castle on the corner of Fourth and Wall, and the Chicago, St. Paul, Minneapolis and Omaha had a less pretentious but still somewhat ornate four-story building at Fourth and Rosabel.

The first depot was the St. Paul and Pacific's small frame building which stood on the east side of

A   *St. Paul's Old Union Depot about 1890.*
B   *The "William Crooks," the St. Paul and Pacific's first locomotive.*
C   *One of the Northern Pacific's St. Paul commuter stations.*

... They hung by their fingertips ...

Sibley, a block south of Third Street and handy to the Lower Landing. West St. Paul had a station near the end of the Wabasha Street bridge. The old warehouse still standing just east of Jackson Street at Shepard Road was another old passenger depot. It served the Milwaukee Road.

In 1879 the railroads joined together to build the St. Paul Union Depot on the site of the St. Paul and Pacific's little depot. A St. Paul landmark for almost 40 years, the depot was a massive Victorian structure that cost $125,000. In 1888, a peak year, 8,000,000 passengers passed through the depot, historian Henry A. Castle reported, and more than 150 trains arrived and departed daily, a figure that seems incredible.

The railroads changed the face of the city. All the roads using the station approached it through the valleys of the four streams that met each other at St. Paul — the Mississippi, the Minnesota, Trout Brook, and Phalen Creek. Tracks into St. Paul crossed the sloughs at the mouth of Trout Brook and Phalen Creek and along the Lower Landing on trestles set on piles, and the Union Depot stood on a pile foundation. Soon, however, the railroad men realized it was more practical to fill in the marshy areas along the river at the Lower Landing. The fill obliterated seven small islands just offshore in the Mississippi, one of them the site of Prince's Rotary Steam Saw Mill. The Trout Brook-Phalen Creek delta also was filled in, leaving only an outlet. Today, miles of trackage cover these areas.

The once lovely residential district extending north of Baptist Hill began to change as industry created or attracted by the railroads, crowded out the homes of the early settlers. Change, of course, had been constant all over the downtown area. Fires, the earliest known form of urban renewal, repeatedly destroyed entire sections of Third Street from the Lower Landing to the Upper Landing.

The city's first major fire in 1850 destroyed the Reverend E. D. Neill's First Presbyterian Church. In 1854 the Pioneer Hook and Ladder Company was organized with thirty-one members equipped with ladders, buckets, axes, and ropes. The next year, the city's fire department was organized, with one hook and ladder wagon. Several citizens also bought a small fire engine. Despite such precautions, fire in 1860 destroyed thirty-four buildings on both sides of Third Street, between Robert and Jackson.

The terror of such fires was vividly described by Helene Mueller Becker in the following reminiscence written, with George A. Rea, for the Fall, 1973, issue of *Ramsey County History.* Mrs. Becker's father and his brother owned and operated a tailor shop on the top floor of a three-story building on the south of Third Street near Wabasha.

"The weather," she wrote, "was cool and windy the afternoon of May 17, 1870. The windows in the shop were closed, the coal burning stove was going strong, and the Mueller brothers, just back from lunch, were busy with their work. One of the brothers opened the window and heard some boys shouting 'Fire! Fire! Fire!' They were pointing to a blazing fire coming from the livery stable next door. Then he noticed that their own building was on fire.

"The brothers . . . saw at once that a thick, black cloud of fumes and smoke was pouring up the stairway. Their only means of escape was on fire. So they ran to the windows facing the steep bluff overlooking the river . . . . The fire department had raced their horsedrawn engines and hook and ladder rig to the site and were placing ladders against the side of the bluff, but the ladders were many feet too short . . . . The two men would have to jump out of the back windows facing south onto the river. It was a drop of eighty feet down the almost vertical sandstone bluff . . . . They hung by their fingertips to the window sills as long as they could. Then . . . they dropped to the slopes below.

"Miraculously, they were not killed. In the meantime, the wind had tossed huge, fiery streamers of burning straw and hay from the livery stable fire onto the houses of squatters who lived nearby along the edge of the Mississippi river,

forcing them to evacuate their possessions.

"The heat from the fire had been so intense that windows were broken and paint blistered on buildings across the street. The building where the Mueller tailor shop was located was damaged so severely it had to be razed."

By the late 1860s, however, the brick and limestone commercial buildings so many older residents still remember were replacing the earlier wooden structures throughout much of the downtown area, and they lined Third Street, the heart of old St. Paul.

The street once was St. Paul's "Great White Way." The St. Paul Gas Light Company was organized March 1, 1856, and gas lights first turned on September 19, 1857, with completion of a gas plant at Fifth and Olive streets. There were seventy-two customers during the first twelve months. The first street lights, fifty in number, were turned on September 1, 1861. One newspaper observed optimistically, "We shall now look for a great decrease of night disturbances." By 1886, gas-lit arches spanned the street from Wabasha to Sibley for such special occasions as State Fair Week and the Winter Carnival.

Third Street was at its peak in the 1870s and 1880s. In 1873 it was the first city street to be paved with pine blocks, which proved to be somewhat less than satisfactory. The *St. Paul Globe* commented, with some exasperation, that "the oldest inhabitant

East Third Street illuminated by gas lights for the Winter Carnival of 1887 or 1888.

A

B

A *High-wheeled bicycles, introduced into St. Paul in 1869 with bike races in Armory Hall. The sport caught on out-of-doors, too, as these two earnest young men demonstrate.*
B *Assumption School, built in 1864 to replace an earlier structure, which burned down in 1863. The first Assumption Church, built in 1856, stands behind the school.*
C *Assumption Church about 1895. With its soaring twin towers, this St. Paul landmark has dominated the city's skyline since the church was completed in 1873.*

has not been able to recall when the pavement was last seen." Buildings lined both sides of the street. Between Wabasha and Jackson there were five banks and most of the city's retail stores. Doctors, lawyers, and architects had offices on the upper floors of the buildings. Theaters and meeting halls clustered around Bridge Square at Third and Wabasha.

St. Paul's Opera House was built in 1867, on the east side of Wabasha between Third and Fourth streets. Parades always marched along Third Street. Velocipede races were introduced in Armory Hall on the third floor of the old Bernheimer Block, the site of today's YWCA. In 1870 the St. Paul Musical Society leased the hall, renamed it Music Hall and held concerts there. Later it became a gymnasium for the St. Paul Gymnastic Society. The Public Library occupied space in the Ingersoll building on Bridge Square.

About 1893 the shopping center moved to Sixth and Seventh streets and commission merchants,

second-hand stores, and employment agencies moved in west of Jackson. This may have been the most picturesque period in Third Street's history. Drays jammed the street, barrels of fruit and other produce were stacked on the sidewalks, railroad laborers and lumberjacks crowded around employment offices, and saloons did a lively business.

The activity was part of the exuberant bustle of these optimistic expansion years. St. Paul was in the midst of a building boom and most of the 19th century buildings still standing in downtown St. Paul were built during this period. In their architecture and ornamentation, they reflect what was happening to people at this time and how they saw themselves.

There are the more ornate structures, such as St. Paul's landmark Assumption Church, built in 1873, in a restrained form of Romanesque; the Endicott building, built in 1889, at 141 East Fourth, in Italian palace architecture; Central Presbyterian

c

Church at 500 Cedar, a combination of Romanesque and Gothic, also built in 1889; the McColl building, at 368 Jackson, another Romanesque design, dated 1890; and First Baptist Church, 499 Wacouta, a Gothic Revival structure, built in 1875.

But there also was a trend toward a more utilitarian style, influenced by such architectural leaders as Louis Sullivan of Chicago. The twelve-story Pioneer Building, St. Paul's first skyscraper, was built in 1889 at 336 North Robert and shows the Sullivan influence. Other buildings that have an ornamented simplicity are Park Square Court at 369 Sibley, built in 1886, and the St. Paul Building at Fourth and Wabasha, built in 1890 as the Germania

The Pioneer building, built in 1889 at 336 North Robert Street. With its twelve stories, it was St. Paul's first skyscraper.

... the most significant incident in the 19th century ...

Bank. Perhaps the most utilitarian of all is the oldest building still standing in downtown St. Paul — the little square Assumption School built in 1864 at 68 Exchange and listed in the Historic American Buildings Survey.

St. Paul's Chamber of Commerce was organized in 1867 with 167 members and James C. Burbank as its first president. In 1884 the Chamber bought land and erected a block at Sixth and Robert streets.

In a healthy business climate, arts and cultural organizations also flourished. The St. Paul Musical Society's orchestra moved its concerts from Music Hall to the opera house. The twenty-two-man organization was the major orchestra in Minnesota during the last half of the 19th century and provided music for both Minneapolis and St. Paul. In 1871 the orchestra introduced Beethoven's Second Symphony at a program dedicating Minneapolis' Academy of Music at Washington and Hennepin avenues.

The Schubert Club's beginnings can be traced to the 1850s and 1860s when people interested in music gathered around a piano in each other's homes to play and discuss music. These meetings evolved into the Ladies Musicale. Afternoon concerts and recitals were held in a hall behind the Ford music store on Third Street between Minnesota and Robert. A few years later, the Ladies Musicale became the Schubert Club. The late John K. Sherman, music critic for the *Minneapolis Tribune*, observed that "the most significant [musical] incident in the 19th century in St. Paul was the founding of the Schubert Club."

America's first musical comedy, *The Black Crook,*

opened in St. Paul in 1867, ran three weeks, and for years was fondly recalled as "St. Paul's first leg show." It was followed by a long series of burlesque operas that packed St. Paul's Opera House. When Mlle. Lamereaux and her "Can Can Dancers from Paris" opened on February 18, 1875, most of the state's legislators were in the capacity crowd and so were the city's councilmen, its mayor and ex-mayor.

Other troupes came to town: "Maggie Leclair's Lovely Ladies" in *The Deamon's Froliques,* a "Teasing, Tasty, Tantalizing, Burlesque!"; "Lilly Clay's Colossal Gaiety Company" in *An Adamless Eden;* " Rose Hill's English Follies"; and "Mlle. Sidonia's Frisky French Favorites."

Scenic spectacles also were an important part of theatrical history during these heady years before motion pictures made them commonplace. *Around the World in Eighty Days* often played St. Paul, and so did *Uncle Tom's Cabin,* one of the greatest of all spectacles. An 1885 production ended in disaster, according to the *St. Paul Globe's* edition for August 30:

"The bloodhounds of an Uncle Tom Company broke loose recently and killed the donkey. The manager, in dire distress, had the donkey's skin removed and sent an actor on in it to impersonate the part, but the accomplished artist, for the first time in his life, failed to make an ass of himself."

Another type of spectacle engrossed St. Paul's citizens in September, 1876. Charley Pitts, a member of the Jesse James gang, was killed by a posse after the bank raid in Northfield, Minnesota. Packed in ice, Pitts' body was carried off to St. Paul and exhibited in the Capitol.

47

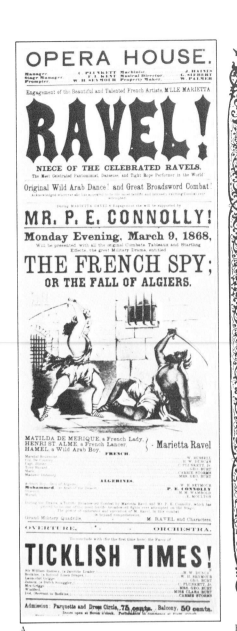

A

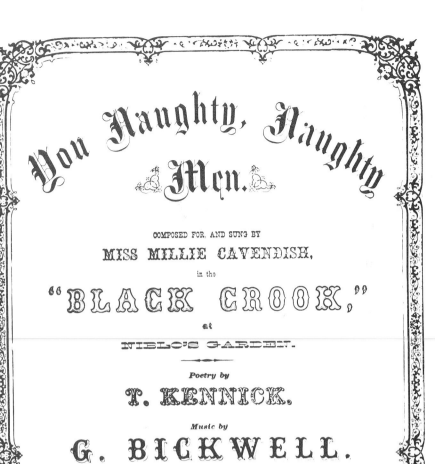

B

C

D

"All us school children were ordered to go and look at that dead man Pitts," one St. Paul resident recalled. "We had to walk by where he lay stript to the waist and that awful bullet hole in his breast."

The body was sold to a St. Paul physician who needed a skeleton and he sank it in a box in Lake Como. When it was discovered, rumors of foul play circulated until the doctor claimed his property. He spread out the bones to bleach in a field at Larpenteur and Snelling. The skeleton next wandered off to Chicago and disappeared. In 1968, however, the author was told that Pitts' bones now repose in a bag in a Shakopee attic.

The James gang had other associations with St. Paul. In *Murder in Minnesota,* author Walter Trenerry places two heavily-armed gang members in St. Paul on August 29, 1876, for an evening of gambling. The next day they bought two horses and disappeared. James and Cole Younger served time at the State Prison in Stillwater, were paroled in 1901 and found jobs in St. Paul — Cole Younger as a tombstone salesman. James Younger, who was 54 by this time, fell in love with 27-year-old Alix J. Mueller, a noted writer who worked for a time for the *St. Paul Pioneer Press.* The state's attorney general refused to permit them to marry while Younger was on parole. Request for a pardon was denied and sick, moody, and despondent, Trenerry writes, Younger killed himself in a St. Paul hotel. Alix Mueller had left St. Paul. She died two years later of tuberculosis.

During the 1870s and 1880s, St. Paul exploded into a city. In the late 1860s the city had less than 15,000 people and only one railroad. Stillwater, White

A

Bear Lake, and Hastings were reached by stage. Few streets were graded, none was paved, and the only sidewalks lay between city hall and the homes of the councilmen.

By 1880 its population was 41,473, and by 1885, 111,397. By 1880, however, Minneapolis' population had outdistanced St. Paul's for the first time in the two cities' uneasy coexistence, and this unpleasant fact of life led to the Great Census War of 1890. On

June 17, 1890, a deputy United States marshal, armed with a warrant charging fraud in taking the Minneapolis census, arrested census-workers in an office at Fourth and Hennepin and picked up six bags of census returns. Evidence for the warrants came from a private detective who said the Minneapolis Bureau of Information told him to pad the census rolls.

"It Means War," *Minneapolis Journal* headlines

B

C

A   *Benjamin Brunson's house at 485 Kenny Road, built in 1855. Brunson and his brother, Ira, made the first survey of the city in 1847. As a deputy United States marshal, Ira Brunson evicted the settlers from the Fort Snelling military reservation in 1840.*

B   *Irvine Park, for many years the center of one of the city's most fashionable residential districts, now St. Paul's first National Historic District.*

C   *John R. Irvine.*

cried. ''The Mask of Hypocrisy Torn from the Malignant Face of St. Paul — A Dastardly Outrage Committed on Minneapolis Citizens by the St. Paul Gang.''

''Arrested!'' the *St. Paul Daily News* trumpeted. ''Scheme to Swell the Population of the Flour City Knocked in the Head.''

Delegations from both cities took their cases to the United States attorney general in Washington, with

A

the result that a new census was ordered. The investigation revealed that both cities had padded their returns. Minneapolis had been more successful at it — adding 18,229 illegal names, including its cemetery "populations." St. Paul had added 9,425, but had been more resourceful. Besides enumerating 325 houses not on the city map, it listed fourteen families as living in the Bank of Minnesota building, twenty-five in a barber shop, 245 in the Union Depot, 120 in one small house, and thirty-five in the Dime Museum. Those connected with the frauds were tried and fined. Even today the 1890 census figures for the two cities are suspect.

During the 1880s, a water system was installed in St. Paul, sewers were laid, streets were paved, and a new courthouse was built. Thousands of homes sprang up in new or expanding neighborhoods.

Pushed out by the spreading wholesale district, Lower Town residents began to move to Irvine Park, Summit Avenue, and Dayton's Bluff. James J. Hill abandoned his graceful, mid-Victorian house at Ninth and Canada for his massive mansion on Summit Avenue. Then, sentimentally, he ordered the Canada Street house torn down.

However, some commercial and industrial firms also were being forced out of downtown, at the same time that immigration into St. Paul was at its peak. Thus, out in these expanding "first ring" neighborhoods were workers who needed jobs and industries who needed workers. The history of these neighborhoods is an interesting chapter in St. Paul's past, particularly since their origins lie in the city's earliest years.

The East Side is a large neighborhood flanking

B

Payne Avenue. Running through the area is the fascinating Swede Hollow. There, Edward Phelan built his claim cabin in 1840 at the head of a ravine where fur traders liked to camp. About 1850 a group of Swedish immigrants settled there, giving it the name of "Svenska Dalen," or "Swede Hollow." They were followed by the Irish, the Italians, the Poles, and, by the 1950s, the Mexican-Americans. At one time Swede Hollow held 60 houses, a grocery, a saloon, and a Catholic Chapel.

In the Lower Payne Avenue neighborhood, between East Seventh Street and Minnehaha, are some of the oldest houses remaining in St. Paul. Benjamin Brunson, who with his brother, Ira, made the first survey of the city in 1847, built the house at 485 Kenny Road in 1855. During the 1880s, working class families flooded into the area, building homes

A *James C. Burbank's mansion at 432 Summit, completed in 1862. Now a National Historic Site, it is owned by the Minnesota Historical Society and is open to the public.*
B *Henry H. Sibley's Italianate mansion at 417 Woodward Avenue.*

with the help of a local building society, finding work among the industrial plants south of East Seventh Street, and shopping along Upper Payne Avenue where 19th century mercantile buildings still stand.

The first settler on Dayton's Bluff, William Evans, the discharged soldier from Fort Snelling who filed his claim in 1839, lived there about twelve years. However, the neighborhood is named for land speculator Lyman Dayton, who settled there in the early 1850s. Stately houses dating from the 1880s still stand on the crest of the bluff. There are

Ferdinand Hinrich's home at 642 East Fifth Street, and Adolph Muench's house at 653 East Fifth Street. The intersection of Earl and Hudson Road was St. Paul's easternmost commercial hub and the half-way point where farmers coming in to market from eastern Ramsey and Washington counties or returning home could stop at the tavern, blacksmith shop, or grocery store. The corner drug store stocked veterinary supplies until the early 1950s.

In the forty-six-acre Mounds Park are six remaining Indian mounds of the sixteen found there by St. Paul's first settlers. The colorful

Commodore William F. Davidson, owner of a fleet of steamboats, among them the *War Eagle*, built his home at 908 Mounds Street. From his cupola he had a long view down the river to Pig's Eye, the old Grand Marais. The house, minus its cupola, now is the Mounds Park Rest Home.

St. Paul's West Side was once technically Spanish territory but occupied until 1851 by the Mdewakanton Sioux. That year George W. H. Bell filed a claim that lay east of the bluffs, near present State Street, and sloped down toward the river. However, the oldest houses still standing on the

General view of St. Paul in 1853:
Catholic Cathedral
Upper Levee   Episcopal Church   Simpson's Dwelling   Baptist Church   Phalen Creek
Steamboat Landing   Court House   Prince's Sawmill   Capitol Building
Dr. Neill's Church   Bridge, Cor. E. Fourth and Jackson Sts.
A.L. Larpenteur's Warehouse   Moffett's Castle

A

B

C

West Side were built in the 1870s. Along Winifred and Ohio streets are old mercantile buildings dating from the 1880s and 1890s and on King Street, between Robert and Livingston, is a block of small brick working-class homes. An old wooden barrel manufactory, one of the few remaining in the United States, has been in the same building at Concord and East Page since 1890. Tucked into the West Side's soft sandstone bluff are the caves once used for growing mushrooms, and for storage — by Yoerg's Brewery, among others. At least two saloons carried on a flourishing trade there.

West Side streets often are steep, sometimes ending in stairways to the next level. A well-known stairway at Hall Street and Prospect Boulevard leads to Prescott Point, named for Charles Prescott, an early settler whose farm lay between Wabasha and Prospect Boulevard. Both Prescott Point and Cherokee Park were favorite spots for a view of the river and downtown St. Paul. Below can be seen

A *Carver's Cave, a drawing by R.O. Sweeney, dated 1867. The Minnesota Historical Society celebrated the centennial of Carver's council with the Indians at the cave by exploring it with boats and candles.*
B *William G. Illingworth's building on Jackson, between Fifth and Sixth streets. A jeweler and clockmaker, he was the father of William H. Illingworth, pioneer St. Paul photographer.*
C *Third Street at Robert during the 1870s. The Pioneer office and printing company is on the right.*

A *Program for a recital at Ford Music Hall, on Third Street between Minnesota and Robert. The Schubert Club's early programs were held here.*
B *Auditorium of the Ford Music Hall.*
C *Bridge Square by gas light, about 1885. Third Street stretches ahead, with Wabasha on the right.*

A

B

C

Harriet Island, named for Harriet Bishop, and what is now Navy Island— once Raspberry Island.

The Upper Landing site at the foot of Chestnut Street across the river also can be seen from Prescott Point. Above the landing is old Upper Town, now the West Seventh Street neighborhood along what once was called Fort Street. Upper Town developed into a fine residential district centered around Irvine Park. One of the city's earliest fashionable neighborhoods, it still has more pre-Civil War houses than any neighborhood in the city. The area around the park is St. Paul's first National Historic District nominated in 1973 for the National Register of Historic Sites by the Ramsey County Historical Society and the Minnesota Historical Society. Governor Ramsey's mansion, built in the early 1870s, also a National Historic Site, is a block from the park. It is owned by the Minnesota Historical Society and is open to the public.

Elsewhere in the neighborhood, one-and-a-half-story structures crowd the narrow streets leading to West Seventh. Apartment and row houses, such as the Lauer Flats at 226 South Western and the Leech Street row houses at 89-95 Leech, were built during the 1880s and 1890s. And along West Seventh is the remnant of the commercial district that has served the neighborhood since 1855 when the Winslow House was built at Seven Corners.

On the bluff above West Seventh Street and actually an extension of Upper Town, is the beautiful Ramsey Hill neighborhood, now part of the Historic Hill District. The two neighborhoods are linked physically by a stairway that climbs the hill from Western to Summit — one of fifty some stairways that once existed throughout the city. John Irvine and Lyman Dayton were the principal landowners in the Ramsey Hill area in the 1850s, when homes began to appear on Summit.

The David Stuart house, built in 1858, is still standing at 312 Summit. In 1862 James C. Burbank finished his two-story mansion at 432 Summit. Now a National Historic Site, it is owned by the Minnesota Historical Society and is open to the public. The Reverend E.D. Neill and Henry M. Rice

61

A

B

A&B *The Lower Levee in 1869 when river traffic was still
at its height. Steamers are the* City of St. Paul *and
the* Minnesota.

. . . built his wonderfully ugly Victorian mansion . . .

also lived on Summit. J.W. Selby, the earliest settler in the neighborhood, had a farm on the site of the Cathedral, and Norman W. Kittson built his wonderfully ugly Victorian mansion on the same site in the 1880s, across the street from James J. Hill's elaborate red sandstone mansion.

By the 1880s, the neighborhood was expanding west of Dale Street and more modest homes were built along Holly, Laurel, Ashland, Portland, and Dayton. Apartment hotels and row houses appeared: the magnificent Riley's Row (Laurel Terrace) at Laurel and Nina, and Summit Terrace, at 587-601 Summit, built in 1887.

The neighborhood declined during the Depression of the 1930s and the post-World War II flight to the suburbs, but both the Ramsey Hill and the Irvine Park Historic districts are now in the middle of an exciting renaissance. The lovely old homes are being restored, many of them by young people who have been buying in the district. Selby Avenue developed as a commercial district in the 1880s and the intersection of St. Albans and Laurel has one of St. Paul's few traffic circles.

North of University Avenue, between Rice Street on the east, Dale Street on the west, and Blair Street on the north, is "Frogtown," settled in the 1880s by working class people who wanted to be close to jobs in the industries and railroad shops along the neighborhood's northern boundary. The origin of Frogtown's name has been hotly disputed and never settled, but it probably had more to do with a marsh in the area, than with its early French settlers. The Germans living in the neighborhood called it "Froschburg"—"Frog City"—very likely a reference to frogs in the marsh.

Houses there are small, on narrow lots. Tacked-on additions are common and some lots have two houses, an arrangement expressive of upward mobility. The owner, in his early, lean years, built a small house. When he had prospered, he moved the small house to the back and built a more substantial house up front.

Frogtown's old commercial and business blocks are disappearing, but a number of corner markets still have fresh meat and vegetable counters, and University Avenue is an active artery of trade.

The North End, lying north of the State Capitol, is bounded on the south by the Burlington Northern

Shops and roundhouse of the First Division, St. Paul and Pacific Railroad, a predecessor of the Great Northern, about 1875. Mississippi Street crosses the ravine on one of the city's pioneer bridges.

... the marvelous, the wonderful, the never-to-be-forgotten little yellow trolleys.

tracks, on the west by Western Avenue, on the east by Jackson Street, and on the north by Maryland Street. It remained farmland until the 1870s when the city annexed the area and houses were built there, many by speculators. Railroad shops along the south edge attracted laborers who settled the neighborhood in the 1880s and 1890s, and some of their houses remain. They are two-story brick or frame houses with pillared front porches. Enough of old Rice Street, the North End's commercial center, remains to suggest the flavor of earlier years.

Until 1887 Lexington Avenue was St. Paul's western boundary. West of Lexington, in rolling pastureland dotted with groves of trees and now-vanished streams and ponds, were a number of early "suburbs" — real estate developments that clustered around their own commercial districts and functioned as separate villages. All were established about the same time — Merriam Park in 1882, Macalester Park in 1883, St. Anthony Park in 1885, and Groveland in 1890. All were served at first by the railroads' "short lines."

Merriam Park was platted by Colonel John L. Merriam who saw the possibilities of a rural village halfway between St. Paul and Minneapolis. He provided for the park which still exists, and the school at Prior and Iglehart. His deeds required that a house cost not less than $1,500 and be completed within a year. Merriam's own house had two stories, a spacious veranda, and square turrets. Rail fare to St. Paul or Minneapolis in the mid-1880s was seven-and-a-half cents, and travel time was about twelve minutes in either direction.

Macalester Park, the oldest residential district in the former Reserve Township, now Highland Park, was platted by a syndicate of Macalester College trustees, including Alexander Ramsey. They purchased Thomas Holyoke's farm, a quarter section between Snelling, Fairview, St. Clair, and Summit, for $150 an acre, gave forty acres to the college, and divided the rest into building lots.

Groveland was created by Archbishop John Ireland who subdivided land surrounding today's St. Thomas College. The land was acquired in 1874 by Bishop Thomas L. Grace who bought 452 acres from William Finn, Reserve Township's first permanent settler. On a small knoll above now-vanished "Lake Mennith," Bishop Grace built a three-story structure for an industrial school that later became the college.

St. Anthony Park was laid out in 1873 by that master landscape architect, Horace William Shaler Cleveland of Chicago. William R. Marshall, governor of Minnesota from 1866 to 1870 and owner of much of the land, engaged Cleveland to map out a suburb of large country estates. Cleveland firmly believed in "adaptation of natural features to the necessities of human occupation and use" and he divided the land with gracefully curved streets that conformed to the slopes of the terrain.

St. Paul was spreading out. For the next 80 years its various parts would be linked in a transportation system that is part of the romance of any city's history — the marvelous, the wonderful, the never-to-be-forgotten little yellow trolleys.

Part Three/The Decorous Decades

The *Pioneer Press* spoke for thousands of approving St. Paul residents when it wrote in 1891 of the city's first electric streetcar line:

"When a man can go from Arlington Hills to Merriam Park for five cents, and from the harvester works near Lake Phalen, to Lake Harriet, on the most distant frontier of Minneapolis territory, for ten cents, he has pretty nearly achieved the maximum of comfort and economy in street railway travel . . ."

The interurban lines carried passengers even farther, to Excelsior, Stillwater, Red Rock, and Inver Grove. This was the streetcar system at its height, replacing the railroads' "short line" passenger stops and adding new lines as the two cities continued their outward sprawl.

It was a colorful era, and it began as early as 1859 when James C. Burbank established the St. Paul Omnibus Lines, consisting of two horse-drawn buses which made trips every half-hour about the downtown district. He also provided omnibuses for theater and church-goers. By 1863 he was running an omnibus to Lake Como three evenings a week during the summer. Round trip was fifty cents.

The St. Paul Street Railway Company was founded on May 9, 1872, with Burbank as president. On July 15 the city's first streetcar, Horsecar No. 1, rumbled forth along a two-mile track running from Seven Corners to the junction of Lafayette and Westminster. Six cars, restricted to a six-mile-an-hour speed limit, gave the line day-long service. Fourteen drivers and thirty horses were needed. Rails were expensive and horses cost $135 to $155. A barn with space for thirty horsecars, 150 horses, and repair and blacksmith shops was built where the Lowry Medical Arts Building now stands.

The earliest horsecars seated fourteen persons on benches which ran along either side of the car. The fare was a nickel and it was dropped into a box at

First "trolley train" in St. Paul. Archbishop John Ireland, second from right, front seat, and Thomas Lowry, on his right, founder of the Twin City Rapid Transit Company, inaugurated the city's first electric streetcar line on February 22, 1890. It ran along Grand Avenue.

A

B

A *Fire Station 11, about 1900, on what was then the southeast corner of Bedford and Beaumont.*
B *Ready for a sail on White Bear Lake. The interurban trolleys brought nearby resort areas within reach of city folk.*
C *Archbishop John Ireland in animated conversation at the Minnesota State Fairgrounds.*

the front of each car. After dark, an evil-smelling oil lamp provided a feeble light. In the winter, a small stove gave off some warmth, and a twelve-inch layer of straw covered the floor. For the driver there were no such amenities. He stood outside on the open platform at the front of the car. Dressed in a buffalo fur coat, felt-lined boots, fur cap, and mittens, he guided his horse, watched for passengers, collected fares and made change. He worked twelve to sixteen hours a day, took twenty minutes off for dinner, was required to wash his car once a day, and was paid $35 per month. Year after year the lines were extended until, by 1887, there were more than forty-five miles of tracks, with 113 cars, 742 horses, and 200 mules.

Hills presented a problem and circuitous routes sometimes were necessary to find grades low enough for a horse or mule to pull a loaded car up a hill. Cable cars were a practical solution, and St. Paul had two lines with double-tracks. One line ran along East Seventh Street from Wabasha to Duluth; the second line ran from Broadway westward and up the Selby Avenue hill.

When cable cars were replaced by streetcars, the hill was still too steep for safety, so a counter-weight car was installed on parallel tracks to offset the weight of the electric car. This system was used until 1907 when the Selby tunnel running under Summit, from Nina to Third Street, was completed at a cost of $415,000.

Electricity opened a whole new era. Pushed by Archbishop John Ireland and Thomas Cochran, a real estate developer, the City Railway Company installed two electric streetcar lines. The first was the Grand Avenue Line, and it began operations on February 22, 1890. The second line ran from Fourth and Wabasha out West Seventh to Cleveland. Both lines served three areas of interest to the archbishop — the developing colleges of St. Thomas and St. Catherine and the St. Paul Seminary.

By 1906 a network of electric streetcar lines had spread throughout Ramsey County and into Washington and Dakota counties. The turn-of-the-century was the heyday of suburban lines whose cars rushed at fifty to seventy miles an hour through the open country to Hastings, White Bear Lake, Mahtomedi, and North St. Paul. For fifty years all streetcars that served the Twin Cities area (as well as many used in other cities) were built in the "car

B

A

barns" at Snelling and University avenues. These
shops built cars that were open on both sides for use
during the summer, had "cow-catchers" for
suburban runs, and were extra wide — nine instead
of eight feet. The first lightweight "noiseless" cars
in the country were made in the Snelling shops
during the 1920s. Many people today have fond
memories of open trolley vestibules with wire gates
where a conductor collected the fare, then pulled a
cord to signal the motorman at the front.

The interurban runs placed nearby resort areas
within the reach of ordinary people, and created
new resorts and playgrounds. White Bear Lake had
enjoyed a national reputation as a resort town since
1853 and by the 1880s summer cottages were being
built there by St. Paul's wealthier citizens. In
describing Manitou Island in 1881, T.M. Newson
remarked, with some candor, that, "It has recently
been purchased by St. Paul and Stillwater
capitalists for a private park and ground for
summer cottages for their own use." The lake did
not remain an enclave for the well-to-do for long. In
1899 the Twin City Rapid Transit Company built
Wildwood Amusement Park. The park had a roller

A *View from the grandstand, overlooking central part
of fairgrounds.*
B *Boating on "Cozy Lake Como," early in this century.*

A

B

A   *Minnesota troops in camp, probably at Camp*
     Meade, during the Spanish-American War.
B   *Minnesota troops leaving Camp Ramsey in 1898, in*
     the midst of a typically gala send-off.

. . . twenty men a day were coming down with the disease.

coaster and merry-go-round, but it is perhaps best remembered for its pavilion and dance hall where bands played for the next forty years.

The new mobility created by the streetcars also linked one of the state's major institutions, the Minnesota State Fair, with both Minneapolis and St. Paul, where it finally settled down. The fair had wandered about central Minnesota for the first thirty years of its existence. It was caught in an epic struggle among cities that hoped to be its permanent location. Fairs were held in Rochester for six years and in Owatonna twice. In 1871, 1872, 1876, and 1879 it was held at Kittsondale, a million-dollar stable and racetrack owned by Norman Kittson near what is now Snelling and University avenues. Colonel William S. King, a flamboyant and irrepressible stock-breeder, was determined to nail down the fair for Minneapolis, where he had promoted an independent exposition for seven years.

Finally, in 1885 a committee, the classic route to compromise, was formed and accepted with loud acclaim and enthusiasm Ramsey County's offer to donate the Ramsey County Poor Farm at Snelling and Como avenues as the site of the fair. For years St. Paul celebrated State Fair Week by lighting up its gas-light arches over Third Street. And the little yellow trolleys on the Como-Harriet line brought fair-goers to the fairgrounds from both Minneapolis and St. Paul.

In April, 1898, when the Spanish-American War began, the fairgrounds were converted into an encampment for the Minnesota infantry regiments, including six companies of St. Paul men, that were mustered into service. One regiment was given the

limited supply of tents and encamped on Machinery Hill. The rest of the men settled down in twelve of the large stock barns. Sanitary facilities were dug, water was drawn from wells on the grounds, and a holiday atmosphere prevailed despite long hours of drill. Sunday was visitors' day. On one Sunday alone, 40,000 people, 15,000 of them from outside the Twin Cities, visited the fairgrounds, renamed Camp Ramsey in honor of the old governor who was still living. They carried baskets of home-cooked food, a welcome relief from the daily diet of boiled potatoes, hardtack, fat pork, and black coffee.

In May the Thirteenth Regiment was ordered to the Philippines, to its delirious delight, and the Twelfth and Fourteenth to a national encampment at Chickamauga, Georgia. The day they arrived in Georgia, the first case of typhoid fever broke out among the Minnesota troops, contracted, without much question, at Camp Ramsey. During the next four months 433 men of the Twelfth — one-third of its muster — developed the disease, and eighteen died. The Fourteenth's records listed 286 ''probable'' cases, with eight deaths.

Meanwhile, the newly recruited Fifteenth Minnesota Regiment moved into Camp Ramsey. Before its muster was completed, typhoid fever broke out and within a month, 180 men were sick. The camp's wells were analyzed, typhoid germs were found, and orders went out to boil all water — orders largely ignored in the summer heat. Tank wagons were disinfected, but still, twenty men a day were coming down with the disease. Next, St. Paul's water, which came from Lake Phalen and Lake Vadnais and was believed to be safe, was trucked into camp. The epidemic continued. The troops

A

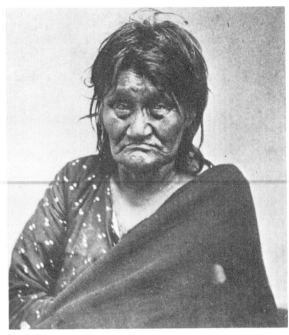

B

received strict orders concerning personal
cleanliness, again largely ignored by men who were
living in the field, and contending with one of the
world's most efficient disease-carriers — the fly.
Twice, all companies were moved to new campsites
on the fairgrounds. Still the disease spread. Almost
400 men were now sick. The camp hospital had been
enlarged again and again and patients were sent
into Minneapolis and St. Paul hospitals. When there
were not enough ambulances, the streetcars
running along the pleasant little interurban line
were pressed into service.

On August 23 the regiment was moved to fresh
grounds at Fort Snelling, but the epidemic did not
die down until late September, after the regiment
moved to Camp Meade, Pennsylvania, a national
assembly point. Of the 1,200 men on the Fifteenth
Regiment's roster, 463 were typhoid fever victims
and twenty died.

The end of the war signaled the beginning of a
relatively tranquil decade. It began auspiciously
with the construction of a new State Capitol
designed by St. Paul architect Cass Gilbert. The
building provided a strong impetus to the

developing artistic community in the state.
Paintings were commissioned for the new Capitol.
A Minnesota artist, Douglas Volk, painted "Father
Hennepin Discovering the Falls of St. Anthony" and
"The Second Minnesota Regiment at the Battle of
Mission Ridge." Nicholas Brewer, another
Minnesota artist who was born in Olmsted County
and studied in New York, produced many of the
governors' portraits now hanging in the Capitol.

The area around St. Paul long had attracted
artists, both professionally trained and self-taught
"primitives." Jonathan Carver had sketched the
Falls of St. Anthony. During the 1830s and 1840s,
Seth Eastman and Edward K. Thomas recorded
scenes around Fort Snelling. Andrew Falkenshield,
who opened a studio in St. Paul in 1856, painted a
portrait of "Old Bets," a Sioux woman from a
distinguished family who was a living landmark in
old St. Paul. Julius Holm caught the inherent
danger and violence of the 1890 Cyclone in his
"Tornado Over St. Paul," painted in 1894. James
Deverreux Larpenteur studied in Paris and in 1886
produced an engaging pen and ink drawing of a
pioneer log cabin in Rose township, north of St. Paul.

74

A *Seth Eastman, a Commandant at Fort Snelling but better-known as one of the great painters of the Mississippi Valley. He served four stints as Commandant, became a Civil War Brigadier General, and left behind him what many experts consider to be the most complete picture by an artist of Indian life in Minnesota.*
B *"Old Bets," a member of a distinguished Sioux family who was a living landmark of old St. Paul. Andrew Falkenshield painted her portrait about 1870, possibly from a photograph.*
C *The State Capitol about 1905. This is the approach toward the Capitol from the north, with Capitol Boulevard in the foreground.*

C

A

B

In 1907 the St. Paul Institute of Arts and Letters was organized as an outgrowth of the St. Paul Academy of Natural Sciences, founded in 1870 and the first organization of its kind in the Northwest. Its original collection, stored in the old State Capitol, was destroyed when the Capitol burned down in 1881. By 1883 new collections were being assembled and these were presented to the Institute's museum. Other scientific specimens were donated, including a mummy shipped from Egypt by a vacationing St.

Paul couple. In 1908 the city leased the three upper floors of the city auditorium on West Fourth Street to the Institute, and a School of Art was established on the top floor and part of the third floor of the building. The Institute also maintained an art gallery in a room provided by the city on the third floor of the St. Paul Public Library. The school's curriculum included life and portrait classes, water color, sculpture, sketching, cartoon and caricature, and handicrafts, such as jewelry, leather work,

76

A *Public baths on Harriet Island, viewed from near the Wabasha Street bridge.*
B *The St. Paul City Hospital, later called Ancker Hospital for its first superintendent, Dr. A. B. Ancker.*
C *A turn-of-the-century teacher in her schoolroom. Classes for students at St. Paul's old Central High School included Latin, French, German, algebra, reading, drawing, civic government, and English composition.*

C

stenciling, wood-block printing, pottery, ceramics, and book-binding.

Interest in crafts, seen today as folk art, had grown beyond the utilitarian toward the artistic embellishment of one's surroundings. Such activity captivated genteel Victorian ladies with time on their hands. Helene Mueller Becker of St. Paul recalled, in a reminiscence written with George Rea for *Ramsey County History,* the fancy work carried in her parents' store, the Mueller Fancy Goods Store

at 191 East Seventh Street.

"Almost all the ladies of a household in those days were accustomed to working with colored silk, woolen knitting materials, or cotton thread," she wrote. "They embroidered designs or monograms on tablecloths, luncheon tray cloths, napkins, pillow cases, and sheets. They knit all sorts of useful garments, especially woolen socks and stockings, caps, and scarves."

During these decorous decades before World

A

B

C

A

B

A *The St. Paul Saints in 1903. Manager Mike Kelley,
   fourth from left, second row, left to manage the
   Minneapolis Millers after the 1923 season.*
B *Nicollet Park, happily labeled "the pillbox" by the
   Saints who played in the more spacious Lexington
   Park. This was standing-room-only during the 1904
   season.*
C *Mike Kelley, manager of the St. Paul Saints for
   twenty-three years.*

C

. . . an eleven-inning game in an hour and forty-five minutes.

War I, the social customs were strictly observed. A woman, Mrs. Becker recalled, did not eat dinner in a public restaurant, such as Carling's Uptown, lest she be considered "fast." Hotel dining rooms were a different matter, for some reason. It was entirely proper for her to have an occasional meal at the Merchants Hotel, or the Ryan, for instance, particularly if she were traveling.

Mrs. Becker also recalled her life as a schoolgirl in St. Paul at the turn-of-the-century:

"It took a half hour to walk from our . . . home [on Dayton's Bluff] to the old Central High School at Minnesota and Tenth," she remembered. "The standard schoolgirl costume consisted of a winter-weight suit of woolen underwear, long black wool stockings, high-button shoes encased in sturdy four-buckle overshoes, and a black or dark blue woolen suit, the skirt having a 'mud flounce' to protect the ankle-length skirt around the edges. Over this . . . . I wore a heavy woolen winter coat that reached to my calves, or an Astrakhan lamb finger-length jacket on more dressy occasions . . . a heavy knitted wool hat or . . . 'Tam-O-Shanter' and a woolen scarf which was long enough to wrap around my neck and then cross over for double protection under my coat. My school books and homework papers were carried in a leather strap fastened with a brass buckle. I always had a nickel in one pocket for 'rain money,' so I could take the horsecar tram if necessary."

Classes were held only in the mornings from 8:30 to 1 p.m. and included Latin, French, algebra, German, English composition, reading, drawing, and civil government. For students taking commercial courses, there were classes in bookkeeping, arithmetic, and penmanship.

Spring brought out St. Paul's cherished sports institution, the St. Paul Saints, a baseball team that played a major part in the life of the city for almost sixty years. In 1901 the club became a charter member of the American Association, along with Minneapolis, Kansas City, Milwaukee, Louisville, Toledo, Indianapolis, and Columbus. For some years the team played at a ballpark downtown, between Robert and Minnesota, Twelfth and Thirteenth streets. By 1910, however, the team was at Lexington Park, at Lexington and University avenues, and there it stayed until the advent of the Twins and big league baseball in 1956.

Those were the years when the Saints could, and did, play an eleven-inning game in an hour and forty-five minutes (three hours today), and each season opened with a parade through Rice Park and downtown St. Paul, before ending up at the ball park. Rivalry between the Saints and the Minneapolis Millers was intense. St. Paul's ball park was one of the biggest in the league, and Saints' fans loved to refer slightingly to the Millers' Nicollet Park as the "pillbox." In Minneapolis, standing-room-only would be in centerfield and any ball that went into the crowd was a two-base hit. In St. Paul, in later years, the roof of the Coliseum ballroom formed part of the left-field fence and home runs hit the Coliseum's roof.

In 1924 the Saints, underdogs of the league that

Celebration of the completion of Northern Pacific's
line to the West Coast. This is East Third Street.

year, won the American Association title by defeating Indianapolis, the Junior World Series by defeating Baltimore, and the minor league championship by out-playing Seattle 12 to 4 in the only game played.

A respectable number of Saints players moved into major league careers. Infielder Charlie Dressen was drafted by Cincinnati, managed Cincinnati, Brooklyn, and Detroit, and led the Brooklyn Dodgers to the National League pennant in 1952 and 1953. Pitcher George Earnshaw was a Philadelphia Athletics star during their championship years of 1929-1931. But perhaps the most illustrious of all was second baseman Miller Huggins who was enshrined in the baseball Hall of Fame in 1964. Huggins managed the New York Yankees from 1918 to 1929. He is remembered as the man who fined Babe Ruth for being overweight.

St. Paul's ball park, of course, was not the only outdoor recreation area in an era when people were beginning to relax. By 1912 St. Paul had eighty parks, squares, boulevards, and playgrounds.

Como Park was created in 1873 when the city bought the lake and land around it for $100,000. The lake, however, was leaking — it once was three times the size it is today — and after much discussion, the city installed a pump system to maintain the water level. There also was a captive labor supply available. The city's workhouse was located in the park and every year about thirty inmates planted trees and shrubs, established grassy lawns and flower beds. Later a lily pond, a Japanese garden, and the pavilion for band concerts were added. The conservatory was completed in 1915.

Of the major parks that were created, some — Central and Summit, Park Place, LaFayette Square — have disappeared. Others, such as Hampden and Carpenter, have been virtually forgotten. Mounds Park and Phalen Park still exist and are widely used, and Harriet Island has been greatly changed.

The island once had, according to Henry A. Castle, "one of the most superb public baths in the country, enjoyed in 1910 by 200,000 bathers." There also was a beach where people swam in the Mississippi, until the 1920s when this was curtailed. The island was, in Castle's words, "covered by shade trees and always tempered by the cool breezes of the river." There were outdoor gymnasiums, refreshment pavilions, and, in an interesting contemporary note, a free day nursery where working mothers could leave their children. And there was a zoo, a hazardous undertaking since the island was repeatedly washed by spring floods. Finally, the zoo was moved to Como Park.

Social service, a practical form of altruism by an immensely practical people, was conspicuous in St. Paul early in the 20th century. Civic leaders were dazzled by the possibilities of the new "playground" movement, an early family-togetherness program formed to promote the "wholesome influence of family life." The city's public playgrounds were created as part of this movement, and by 1912 there were a dozen recreation fields, one of them a large tract of land on Lexington near the present Central High School.

The Protestant Orphan Asylum occupied a house and grounds on Marshall Avenue. The county's almshouse and poor farm, now the Ramsey County Fairgrounds, had been relocated on White Bear Avenue in North St. Paul. The St. Paul City Hospital, under the management of Superintendent A.B. Ancker, the city and county physician, had grown into a 615-bed hospital from its humble beginnings in an old stone residence, where water came from a well, kerosene lamps supplied light, operations were performed behind a screen, and the cellar was the morgue.

A

A *Wholesale district along Third Street. Produce is piled up on the sidewalks as horse-drawn wagons with their drivers wait to load up. Presley's was at 102 East Third Street.*
B *Metropolitan Opera House on Sixth Street. St. Paul was a major stop for touring theatrical companies.*
C *Panoramic view of St. Paul, from Marlborough Flats.*

B

In 1907 the Young Men's Christian Association built its "stately edifice," a building that still stands at Ninth and Cedar streets. That same year the Young Women's Christian Association was organized in St. Paul. In 1911 the YWCA erected a building at Fifth and Auditorium streets.

Names chosen by some of the early organizations often reflected a firm grasp of purpose. The Society for the Relief of the Poor grew out of an older organization called the Society for the Improvement of the Poor. In *James J. Hill and The Opening of the Northwest*, author Albro Martin gives a heart-warming account of Hill and the Society in 1909 and 1910. Morgan L. Hutchins, the Society's secretary,

C

A

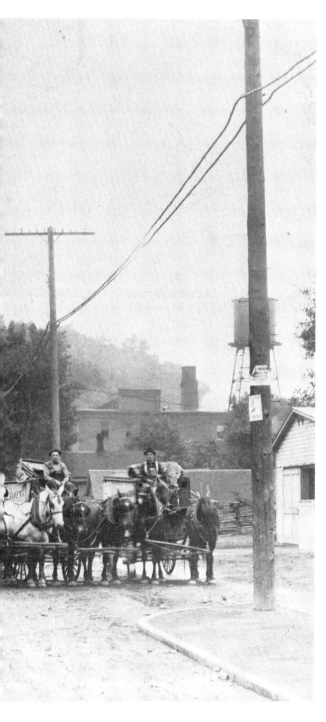

B

A *Delivery truck lineup in front of Yoerg's Brewery.*
B *Label from Yoerg's beer, made by one of St. Paul's*
   early breweries.

A

B

A *Dr. C. M. Cannon in his 1910 Pierce Arrow. Rice Park and the Old Federal Courts Building are in the background. The old Orpheum Theatre is on the right.*
B *St. Paul's best-known and most notorious "house of ill-fame." It was erected in 1888 by a young woman whose name was Hanna Steinbrecker but who was better known as Nina Clifford. She apparently was a woman of style, since much local lore swirls about her and her house in the center of St. Paul's "under the hill" red light district, an area around Hill and Exchange streets below the bluff where the Civic Parking Ramp now stands.*
C *James J. Hill, a candid photograph of the Empire Builder strolling along the streets of downtown St. Paul.*

Hill's death . . . signaled the end of an era.

C

traveled daily about St. Paul in a small, covered van pulled by an old horse, carefully checking out each appeal for help and bringing deserving cases to the attention of Hill and other wealthy donors. Hill offered to replace Hutchins' old horse with a handsome young horse from his North Oaks farm, but Hutchins refused. Such a gift, he felt, would be far too elegant, far too spirited, and therefore, far too out-of-keeping with the skill and tact he felt was necessary in helping people.

Hill's death in 1916 signaled the end of an era. He was among the last of that spectacular group of young men who had settled in St. Paul in the 1850s and built their fortunes around the growth of the city and its hinterland.

Hill had reorganized the St. Paul, Manitoba and Pacific Railroad into the Great Northern and acquired operating control of the bankrupt Northern Pacific. This concentration of control over the northwestern railroads led to one of the stormiest episodes of his life, the now legendary

collision in 1901 and 1902 between Hill, backed by New York financier J.P. Morgan, and E.H. Harriman of the Union Pacific. Both Hill and Harriman wanted control of the Burlington. The ensuing struggle hinged on control of Northern Pacific stock. Harriman attempted to buy it, in competition with Hill and Morgan. It was a close fight, one that had a disastrous effect upon the stock market. Many speculators who had sold N.P. shares short had to cover their sales with shares that soared in price as the Hill-Harriman bidding rose.

It was time, President Theodore Roosevelt decided, to invoke the Sherman Antitrust Act. When the government won its subsequent antitrust action, Hill and Harriman worked out a solution. Hill retained control of his roads, and Harriman was given a seat on the Northern Pacific and Burlington boards, and on the board of the Northern Securities Company, a holding company Hill had created. Railroad stock acquired in the struggle was to be converted into Securities Company stock. The

B

A

A *"The most elegant train running between St. Paul and Chicago." That, at any rate, is how the Burlington described its "Limited."*
B *The automobile edges out the horse and buggy in this prophetic scene on Sixth Street, east of St. Peter, about 1915.*
C *Fire-fighters and their first gasoline pumper, acquired in 1913. Terrifying fires repeatedly destroyed the buildings throughout the city.*

resulting litigation began in St. Paul's Old Federal Courts Building, where Hill and his attorneys, all St. Paul men, spent long hours in testimony in the courtrooms. Eventually, the United States Supreme Court ordered Northern Securities dissolved.

St. Paul, the center of Hill's enterprises, was bursting with pride and energy by 1916 when its civic leaders, headed by his son Louis W. Hill, decided to revive the Winter Carnival. It had been founded in 1886 to demonstrate that St. Paul was, too, habitable in winter after a visiting New York newspaperman had declared in print that it was not. One of the most spectacular features of the Carnival's earlier years was the Ice Palace. In 1888 the palace was a turreted structure 144 feet tall, and 120 feet wide, with a 100-foot central tower. It covered an acre. More than 20,000 blocks of ice, most of them cut from Lake Como, were used. Electric

C

A *Toboggan slides, without which no Winter Carnival would be complete. A favorite through the years has been the slide that started at the present State Capitol and ran down St. Peter into downtown St. Paul.*

B *St. Paul's Winter Carnival ice palace in 1887, illuminated from inside with electric lights.*

B

A

lights illuminated the palace from inside its walls.

Toboggan slides were another Carnival feature. In 1886 there were six. A favorite of all the Carnivals was the slide that started at the site of the present Capitol and ran down Cedar Street into downtown. Three "carnival clubs," the Wacouta, Nushka, and Windsor, built a 500-foot slide down Crocus Hill. Dayton's Bluff had two slides. In 1916 and 1917 there was a big two-chute slide down Ramsey Hill from Summit. Etiquette required that the toboggan steerer not advance his head nearer than fifteen inches toward the shoulders of the lady seated in front of him. How the toboggan was to be steered from behind was not explained.

The Carnival had its own song books with such ditties as "To-bog-i-og-i-og-gan!" and, "Soop Her Up, Tee High!," and the parades marched to the "Minnesota and Northwestern Rail Road Triumphal Grand March." Railroads cut their fares to lure visitors to St. Paul.

Curling matches drew immense crowds, and the ancient Scots game became a favorite social sport still popular in St. Paul. But the parade was the highlight, and it is easy to understand why, from this early rhapsodic description:

"Stately-stepping steeds; champing their bits; tossing their proud heads . . . drawing superb sleighs of every graceful shape, filled with pretty women enveloped in furs . . . . The sleighs swiftly glide over the packed snow on the streets . . . . Silvery laughter floats above the frosty air . . . . It is one of the grand features of the winter fete."

Some of the carnival clubs became permanent social organizations. Formed as a toboggan club, the Nushka Club organized snowshoe tramps to Merriam Park and back again to a rendezvous at the "Lookout," on Ramsey Hill at Summit. A skating rink at Summit and Western furnished a new sport. It was but a short step to informal "Saturday Nights," summer coaching parties, New Year's Eve masquerades, Valentine parties, the purchase of a clubhouse, and the consignment to oblivion of the old tobogganning parties.

By June of 1916, some of the young men among the carnival revelers found themselves on the Mexican border in Texas. Minnesota's National Guard regiments were called into federal duty to help deal with Francisco (Pancho) Villa's raids into American territory. The regiments included the First Minnesota Infantry, with five companies of St. Paul men, and the First Regiment of Field Artillery, with two batteries from St. Paul. Company quarters were

A

B

A *Winter Carnival revelers "mobilizing" at the Town and Country Club in 1917.*

B *St. Paul's Curling Club, 1910. This ancient Scots game drew immense crowds during the early Winter Carnivals and became a favorite social sport.*

A

A *"Farewell"* — *World War I.*
B *Draftees from St. Paul leaving for service in World War I.*

B

in the St. Paul Armory on Exchange and West Sixth Street, a four-story brown sandstone building completed in 1904 and fondly remembered by St. Paul citizens who attended dances in its assembly hall on the top floor.

In the early winter of 1917 there was no question but that the United States soon would be involved in the war in Europe. After war was declared on April 6, 1917, twelve draft boards were set up in Ramsey County, as well as a district appeal board to rule on disputed draft cases.

With the outbreak of war, several units volunteered as a group. A Hamline University ambulance unit was the first to leave the state, when it departed in June for training at Allentown, Pennsylvania. Shortly afterward, Base Hospital 26,

made up chiefly of men from St. Paul and Minneapolis, was sent to Fort McPherson, Georgia, and then overseas.

On June 23 the First Minnesota Artillery was mobilized at Fort Snelling. Redesignated the 151st Field Artillery, it was the only Minnesota regiment to go through the First World War almost intact. It had originated in St. Paul as the Emmet Light Artillery Regiment, a state militia unit organized in 1881.

In September, 1917, the regiment was ordered to Camp Mills, New York, where it became part of the elite Forty-second, or Rainbow Division, and it served at Chateau-Thierry, through the Champagne Defensive, the Marne, and St. Mihiel. A graphic picture of these men in action at St. Mihiel has been

A

A *Red Cross workers meeting the troop trains at the old Union Depot during World War I.*
B *St. Paul's Red Cross Motor Corps. Members are Mrs. Robert Peet, Mrs. Lewis Shaw, Mrs. Carl Smith, Mrs. Jule Hannaford, Mrs. Milton Lightner, Mrs. H. L. Donahower, Mrs. Sam Magoffin (at the wheel), Josephine Sweeny, Mrs. Philip Carpenter, and Alice Warren.*
C *Knitting for the Red Cross during World War I. Women pledged themselves to knit a pair of socks every week for ten weeks in response to the St. Paul Red Cross' request for 9,000 pairs of socks monthly.*

left by Louis L. Collins in his history of the regiment.

At 1 a.m. on September 12, 1918, the artillery opened fire to prepare the way for the infantry. After four hours of barrage, the men climbed out of the trenches to begin their advance.

"At the same time, the light artillery raised its fire," wrote Collins, "and the line of falling steel swept slowly along toward the north, progressing at the predetermined rate of 100 meters in four minutes."

After the Armistice, the regiment remained in Europe as part of the Army of Occupation. In April, 1919, the men were ordered home.

In St. Paul, the war years were characterized by an outburst of patriotic fervor. The St. Paul chapter of the American Red Cross encouraged women to knit socks for soldiers and the *St. Paul Pioneer Press* published a pledge for them to sign:

"In response to the Red Cross request for 9,000

B

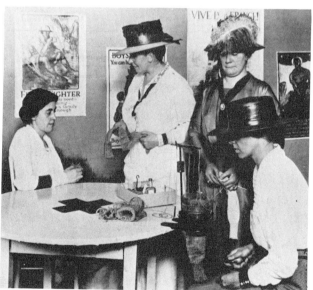

C

pairs of socks from St. Paul monthly, I agree to produce one pair a week for ten weeks. When I start work, I am to receive a Sock Service Sign to hang in my window, and I am to be allowed 14 hours credit for each pair, toward earning Red Cross emblems and stripes. I understand that I am to draw yarns through the nearest working unit when I am advised of its location."

Families coped with food shortages. Sugar was rationed. "Beginning this week," the *St. Paul Pioneer Press* announced in July, 1918, "the State Food Administration has ordered that persons who wish sugar for canning may no longer purchase the 100 pounds previously allowed." Wheat flour also was in short supply, and women were urged to make their bread with rye, barley, or potato flour. St. Paul's YWCA taught classes on making bread without white flour, making surgical dressings, making-over clothing, canning and automobile work. Telegraphy classes were organized to train

women to fill jobs left by men who had gone to war.

This was, however, a sad period in St. Paul's history and a hysterical period in American life, with bizarre and unfortunate consequences. Intense patriotism was accompanied by a violent surge of public opinion against everything German. Victims of the persecution that followed in St. Paul were not only citizens of German birth or ancestry, but anyone who had shown sympathy for the German and Austrian governments, as well as anyone who doubted the wisdom of America's entry into the war. Much of this patriotic zeal was reflected in the work of the Minnesota Public Safety Commission which was approved by the state legislature on April 16, 1917, and given almost dictatorial authority for defense and for support of the war effort.

Commission members were well-intentioned but they were prone to issue from their St. Paul headquarters such bulletins as this:

"It is said by a writer that one out of every twenty persons in the nation today is disloyal and about one out of every one hundred is so openly seditious that he should face a firing squad if he were to receive the sort of punishment that is meted out by any autocratic government. Anyone who talks and acts against the government in time of war, regardless of the 'Constitutional right of free speech' which has been so sadly abused, is a traitor and deserves the most drastic punishment."

Such declarations had the predictable results. Neighbor informed on neighbor, sometimes spurred by petty rivalries and feuds. Such an avalanche of

A *World War I "loyalty parade."*
B *"Germania" comes down from her pedestal. During the anti-German frenzy of World War I, Germania Life Insurance Company officials took down this life-size cut marble figure which had ornamented the building on Minnesota Street at Fourth. Even the building's name was changed, in 1918, to the Guardian Building. It was razed in the early 1970s.*

A

B

A

B

102

A *Women's suffrage rally in Rice Park, 1914.*
B *Striking streetcar employees marching in
   downtown St. Paul. Defying a ban against strikes,
   motormen walked out in 1917 and Home Guard units
   kept order during the rioting that followed.*

. . . downtown streets rang with the shouts of the mob.

letters reporting highly suspicious persons poured into St. Paul that the Commission set aside February 26-27, 1918, as Alien Registration Days. Lest they be considered disloyal, many St. Paul Germans joined in the spy-hunt. A German priest from Assumption parish reported eight Oblate Fathers who recently had arrived in the archdiocese, and asked the archbishop to remove them.

A Home Guard was formed to replace National Guardsmen who were away in federal service. The 400 men in St. Paul's three units were assigned to investigate sections of the city and check draft registration cards of men suspected of being ''slackers.'' German parishes were particularly vulnerable. Home Guardsmen, working block-to-block, paid special attention to pool halls, saloons, rooming houses, and cheap hotels. Guards stood at the exits until everyone had been examined, and all men between the ages of 21 and 32 who could not produce draft registration cards were sent to the St. Paul Armory.

The *St. Paul Pioneer Press* reported a ''slackers'' raid on July 7, 1918:

'' At 9:30 P.M. the Home Guards . . . went out in details to cover assigned districts. Those going longer distances went in automobiles. The first person to be turned in was H.J. Warnock, 105 South Finn Street.

'' 'Today was the first day in months that I omitted carrying my registration card,' Warnock protested. 'I should have known better. I went down to the depot to buy a railroad ticket and —

zip — I'm pinched.' ''

There was a rush to eliminate the study of German from public schools, with the unfortunate result that, in time, study of all foreign languages was curtailed. The Germania Life Insurance Company in St. Paul hauled down the statue of ''Germania'' from above its Fourth Street entrance. Sauerkraut became ''liberty cabbage,'' dachshunds, ''liberty hounds;'' German fried potatoes, American fries; and hamburger, Salisbury steak.

The Home Guard had other duties. Streetcar motormen, defying a ban, went out on strike in October, 1917, and Home Guard units were called in to keep order when rioting by mobs numbering in the thousands, according to the excited newspaper accounts, stopped trolley service.

'' A score of persons were injured,'' the newspapers reported. '' Eleven men were arrested. Scores of street car windows were smashed. Absolutely uncontrolled, wild crowds tied up the street car system of the city . . . . Conductors and motormen were stoned from cars and ran to save themselves as the anger of the throngs vented itself on the property of the Twin City Rapid Transit Company . . . . Stranded cars, their sides battered and their panes of glass demolished, were deserted on downtown corners. For four hours . . . the downtown streets rang with the shouts of the mob.''

Car crews were captured by the rioters at Fourth and Robert, Fourth and Wabasha, and Seventh and Robert streets. Chief of Police J.J. O'Connor assigned thirty officers to ride some of the suburban

A GRATEFUL PEOPLE PAUSE IN THEIR WELCOME
TO THE VICTORIOUS LIVING TO PAY SILENT
TRIBUTE TO THE ILLUSTRIOUS DEAD.

A

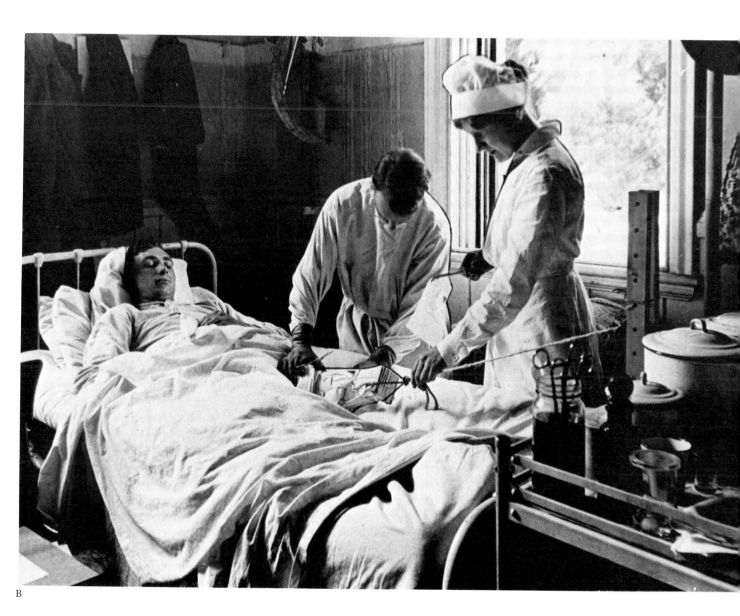

B

cars. Finally, the Home Guard units established order.

In the autumn of 1918, health officers in St. Paul were watching with concern the spread of Spanish influenza throughout the state. From Camp Grant, Illinois, where he was stationed, Dr. Egil Boeckmann of St. Paul, a member of the state health board, warned physicians that the disease "spreads like fire, very severe in onset and very prone to complications of Lobar Pneumonia. . . . I want to impress upon the Board that you are dealing with the most serious epidemic of any kind you have ever been up against."

CHIFFON VEILS ARE WORN AS INFLUENZA MASKS ON STREET

"It's a Halloween prank."

"No, they are going to a masquerade party."

The above were some of the comments overheard Thursday when a group of women appeared on Summit avenue on their way to an informal tea. They wore influenza masks. Since then these masks have been adopted by many persons.

Many women are wearing chiffon veils as a street mask, changing to the gauze kind when doing Red Cross and other relief work.

The demand for face masks is so great that it is not possible for the Red Cross to furnish all. The following instructions for making a mask at home is timely. These directions are direct from Red Cross headquarters:

"From gauze, thirty-six inches wide, cut forty-three inches on sal vage. Divide in four strips each, nine ir Fold strips into half lengthwise, then inte Do not turn in salvage. Stitch four s pleats on both seven-inch ends. Attach each corner. Place black thread in cen

A The wedding of Miss Mabel Cooper, daught
lly avenue, and Dr. William
nlace at 12 M., yesterday a
an officiating.
endants and the
immediate
e home
e frier
Mrs

To regain health and strength after Spanish Influenza or Pneumonia

BUILD up your blood and body with Gude's Pepto-Mangan.

The germs of Spanish Influenza or Pneumonia are very devastating in their effect. Your blood is impoverished, your vitality drained to low ebb, your powers of resistance so enfeebled that any serious chronic disease may fasten on you.

To completely regain your health and strength, you must restore your blood to normal richness and redness. Gude's Pepto-Mangan is a wonderful general tonic and blood builder. It increases the number of the red blood cells and their capacity to carry oxygen to every cell and tissue, charging your system with new strength, energy and resistance to disease. It increases the appetite, is promptly assimilated, and exceedingly pleasant to taste. Endorsed and prescribed by the medical profession for over 25 years.

Gude's Pepto-Mangan also is of great value in the *prevention* of Spanish Influenza or Pneumonia. It makes rich, red, pure blood—your best fortification against the inroads of sickness.

FRIENDLY WARNING No. 1:—Don't try to doctor yourself for such acute and dangerous diseases as Spanish Influenza or Pneumonia. Even at the first sign of a cold in the head, call in a physician. This precaution may save your life.

FRIENDLY WARNING No. 2:—There is only one Pepto-Mangan and that is Gude's. Sold in bottle and package as here shown. For sale at all drug stores.

Study this picture so you will know how Gude's Pepto-Mangan looks.

Gude's Pepto-Mangan
"The Red Blood Builder"

Is made only by M. J. BREITENBACH CO., Manufacturing Chemists, New York

B

A *The ingenuity of women. Chiffon masks replaced gauze for social occasions at the height of the influenza epidemic.*
B *Patent medicine and the influenza crisis. The Spanish influenza epidemic of 1918 is still recalled with dread.*

The committee was authorized to take the necessary steps . . .

By November 1, 1918, St. Paul had 3,031 cases of influenza, with 1,946 people under quarantine, and a Citizens' Committee was formed to meet the new crisis.

"Immediate provisions of a 300-bed influenza hospital, with the taking over of the YWCA building and equipping it at an estimated cost of $30,000 was authorized by the Citizens' Committee at the City Council chambers yesterday," the *St. Paul Pioneer Press* reported on November 1. "The committee, of which Louis W. Hill is chairman, was authorized to take the necessary steps to provide the free public hospital at the city's expense . . . ."

Drastic restrictions were placed on the use of churches, soda fountains, and saloons, but the wild demonstrations on Armistice Day, with crowds milling about the streets, spread the disease further. Newspapers published instructions on how to care for the sick:

"Used dishes must be boiled. Linen, towels, etc., must be kept separate and boiled. To kill the germs, keep the house clean with plenty of soap and water, let in plenty of sunlight . . . . Sleep and rest in a cool, airy room is the best that can be done for a patient."

People were advised to wear face masks of surgical gauze, and business firms began to hand them out to their employees after a group of Summit Avenue women made masks fashionable by wearing them to a tea.

"The St. Paul Gas Light Company asked [the Citizens' Committee] for 1,500 [masks] and the American Hoist and Derrick Company wanted 1,500," the *St. Paul Dispatch* reported. "In view of the shortage of masks, all those institutions employing women are asked to call at the Citizens' Committee headquarters and get a sample mask, having their women make their own masks . . . . Many women are wearing chiffon veils as a street mask, changing to the gauze kind when doing Red Cross and other relief work." Plans were made to have streetcar windows closed, and their transoms provided with cloth protectors.

Advertisers naturally addressed themselves to the epidemic.

"To regain health and strength after Spanish Influenza or Pneumonia, build up your blood and body with Gude's Pepto-Mangan." And, to cover all bases — "Gude's Pepto-Mangan also is of great value in the prevention of Spanish Influenza. It makes rich, red, pure blood — your best fortification against the inroads of sickness."

The first decades of the 20th century were drawing to a close. They were decorous decades, despite agitation for change that could be seen in St. Paul, as elsewhere. Such issues as women's suffrage, Prohibition, and labor unrest, simmering under the surface during the war years, would rise to the top and profoundly change American life.

107

Part Four/Prohibition, Prosperity, Panic

Nowhere, perhaps, can the 20th century's great social movements — suffrage, prohibition, social service — be seen more clearly than in St. Paul and in the work of the city's women, a phenomenon that was recognized all over the country.

In the 19th century, Edith R. Mabie of St. Paul could write:

"I don't think it worthwhile to say anything about myself. Never have amounted to very much except as a wife and mother in which capacity I hope I have not been an entire failure judging by results."

This "little brown dove" image of what the pious Victorians fondly believed to be the True Woman bore little resemblance to St. Paul's sturdy, vigorous women in either the 19th or the 20th century. The record of their contributions to the city's history is breathtaking in inventiveness and enthusiasm. In 1867 twelve women met at First Presbyterian

Church to found the "Home for the Friendless," which gave temporary shelter to poor immigrants who were crowding into St. Paul, and particularly to women and children. Out of this grew the Protestant Home of St. Paul, the oldest home for the aged in Minnesota.

As the years passed, St. Paul's women organized Children's Health Days, opened milk stations in schools to provide children with free milk, formed Mothers' Clubs that grew into Parent-Teacher Associations, taught Americanization classes, established more than thirty public drinking fountains throughout the city, and organized classes to teach the needy how to sew their own clothing.

Some of their activities were surprisingly contemporary. They worked for prison reform and freedom for political prisoners, promoted the beautification of the city through the planting of trees and shrubbery, protested the high cost of living and sought solutions for it, worked for highway improvements, opposed the death penalty, supported indeterminate sentencing, and backed a Duluth-St. Lawrence Seaway — all before 1920.

Of the 550 Minnesota women listed in a *Who's*

The NRA's Blue Eagle in a St. Paul window.

LES RECORD, CLOSING PRICES AND YEAR'S RANGE OF

Large Financial Interests, Still Uneasy Over Future of the Market, Hold Aloof From Making Purchases, Feeling That Public Selling Will Go On

New York Journal of Commerce Special Financial Service to the Pioneer Press.

New York, Oct. 4.—After recovering to some extent from the severe break of the previous day, another wave of liquidation forced stock exchange prices down to new low ground. Impairment of the marginal position was chiefly responsible for the new setback, which reached its greatest intensity just before the close, when United States Steel sold at 206½, after selling as high as 215 earlier in the day.

Large financial interests have not changed their attitude towards the market future. They continue to keep aloof from making extensive purchases for the most part, feeling that public selling will continue for some little time yet. After the marginal position has been corrected and weak holders eliminated, any major recovery would depend on improvement in the business outlook. Steel, automobile, building, oil, copper and several other industries face a rather uncertain outlook, and stocks in these groups may be slow to rally on any large scale, although in individual instances they may benefit materially.

On the other hand, those groups of securities which will be benefited by favorable business developments may rally from current levels within a short time. This applies to all individual companies, no matter what the industry, which have been able by new developments to cut the cost of production and increase profits by new products. Also it applies to those industries like utilities, railroads and merchandising companies where merger developments or an upward trend in volume of business are expected shortly.

NEW YORK STOCK PRICE AVERAGES FOR DAY AND YEAR

New York, Oct. 4—Total stock sales today, 5,623,900; previous day, 4,747,330; week ago, 4,597,590; year ago, 4,336,200; January 1 to date, 836,570,760; year ago, 627,193,300; two years ago, 415,993,500.

Average Stock Prices	Friday	Thursday	Week Ago	Year Ago	1929 High	1929 Low
50 Industrials	225.1	227.3	235.3	182.3	252.8	201.7
50 Railroads	149.8	151.2	154.6	121.9	167.8	128.6
20 Utilities	309.0	313.1	340.3	159.5	353.1	193.1

KEY TO TABLE. XD—Ex-dividend; XR—Ex-rights; AS—Actual sales; A—Plus Extras; B—Including extras; D—Partly stock; F—2½% quarterly in common stock; H—Paid so far this year; K—Payable in stock; N—Payable 1-40 of a share in Class A stock quarterly; 1929 range given to show comparison for this year. Annual dividend rate in dollars per share is shown following name of stock.

A

Who of Minnesota Women, published in 1924, 143 were from St. Paul. Among them were women like Minnie Fay Hessian, a St. Paul policewoman appointed in 1913, who inspected dance halls and public places of amusement, adjusted cases of domestic difficulty, helped runaway girls, and found homes for unmarried mothers. Eliza Thompson Edgerton Newport founded St. Paul's first coffee house where food and coffee were sold at cost, and helped establish a houseboat at the Lower Landing that was the first mission in America to offer low-priced clean lodgings to working-men. Mary Francis Fox Kordosky bought, furnished, and sold apartment buildings, became a railroad inspector and, in 1923, deputy sheriff of Ramsey County, the first woman in Minnesota to hold such an office.

\FTER CRASI

12,894,680 SHARES CHANGE HANDS IN SALES STAMPED TICKER 4 HOURS BEHII

*IL
\GS*

Despite Heavy Volume of Early Distress Selling V ous Rally at Close Indicates There Is Little Gr for Prolonged State of Uneasiness, Financial Le Assert After Conference.

TRADERS CHEER AS U. S. STEEL, OLD-TIME BAROMETER, TURNS UP CHECKING PLU

New York, Oct. 24.—(P)—The remarkable era of avid speculation in stocks which has swept over the country duri past five years came to a climax today in the most terrifying ede of selling—totaling 12,894,680 shares—ever experienced New York Stock Exchange and other leading security markets

The sickening plunge was checked late in the session when States Steel common, old-time barometer of the market, turn ward and was greeted by exultant cheering.

Not since the war panic which resulted in closing the ex for seventeen weeks in 1914 has Wall street seen such a da trying day and never in financial history have security market thrown into such a tumult. It appeared for a time that the markets would be unable to face the situation and that trading have to be suspended but the leading exchanges saw the through, although a few floor traders collapsed and had to be from the trading floors.

CURB TRADING ALSO SPECTACULAR.

Trading on the New York Curb Exchange was also spec and the total volume was 6,148,300 shares, a new high compared with the previous record of 3,715,400 shares, Monday. Sales of Cities Service common broke the one issue, reaching 1,151,900

Standard dividend nav'

with the more spec
would bring in blo
floor of the sto

*ders and
, Too,*

Paul were
fter dark
ry as the
han four
es. Never
offices in
I through-
g room at
n of the

e sustain-
was con-
by the St.
uring part
tape was
recording
erence was
ed stock

B

A *The ominous break in the stock market in early October, 1929, that led to the Crash of 1929 and the Great Depression.*

B *The terrifying stampede of selling on October 24, 1929, that began the Crash of '29.*

Mabel Hansen Guise successfully lobbied bills through the legislature to put women on juries and establish a fifty-four-hour work week for women in industry. Elsa Redeker Obst was elected treasurer of Ramsey County in 1922, the first woman to hold such an office. Harriet Warner Schoonmaker was appointed secretary of the state's minimum wage commission in 1921. Sophie Greve Kenyon, actively engaged for thirty years in buying and selling stock, also found time to organize the Woman's Welfare League, the first large suffrage club in Minnesota, and served on the board of the National Woman's Party.

A common thread runs through the backgrounds of these women, in addition to their work for women's suffrage as members of such organizations

A   *Franklin Delano Roosevelt campaigning in St. Paul in 1932. He spoke at the auditorium on April 18 to the largest dinner gathering held in the Northwest up to that time.*
B   *Hopelessness of the Depression. Men begged for food at back doors throughout the city and slept on its park benches during the worst Depression in the nation's history.*

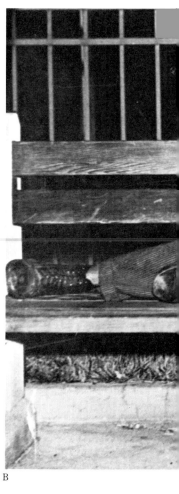

B

A

as the Equal Franchise of St. Paul. A majority of them also supported Prohibition through the Women's Christian Temperance Union, which had an active franchise section. With Mrs. Kenyon as chairman, a large suffrage rally in Rice Park in 1914 attracted much attention, and on September 8, 1919, when the state legislature ratified the Nineteenth Amendment, the women celebrated with a "Jubilee Banquet" at the St. Paul Hotel. They already had celebrated the advent of Prohibition when the Eighteenth Amendment was ratified in January, 1919.

There were gloomy predictions that Prohibition would create widespread law-breaking, but, during the Jazz Age of the 1920s, people paid little heed. They were too busy having a good time. The

Lexington Pavilion at Lexington and University avenues advertised "25,000 feet of dancing floor smooth as glass" with music by "Wally Erickson's famous dance band" and the latest fox trots and one-steps. Dances costing fifty cents for gentlemen and twenty-five cents for ladies were held on Saturday, Sunday and Wednesday evenings.

Downtown, Norma Talmadge might be seen at the Capitol theater in a sizzler like "Within the Law," playing on a bill with Stan Laurel in "Under Two Jags." As early as 1923, during a heat wave, the Capitol reminded its customers that, "Our cooling system is operating to keep you cool while you enjoy a restful program in a comfortable opera chair." Matinees cost twenty-seven cents.

St. Paul had a "Better Homes Week" from June 4

A

B

C

A *Young pickets during the Depression. Mayor Mark
   H. Gehan was booed during the Workers Alliance
   protest against relief cuts. Frank Rarig was director
   of Ramsey County Welfare and the first organizer of
   the WPA program.*
B *Farmers crowd into the Capitol in demand for
   relief. More than 20,000 massed at the Capitol on
   March 22, 1933, while their leaders asked a joint
   session of the legislature for tax relief, aid for
   debtors, and a moratorium on mortgages and
   evictions.*
C *A street-sweeper in downtown St. Paul during the
   1920s.*

A

A *NRA parade along Sixth Street in August, 1933.*
B *Kellogg Boulevard in 1933, Robert to Wabasha
   streets. The stretch of boulevard on the right is what
   remained, at that time, of old Third Street.*

B

to 10, 1923. Its aim, according to the General Federation of Women's Clubs, was "to direct the family life back into the home channels, to increase the efficiency of the home, to relieve the drudgery of the housekeeper and to stimulate the cultural and aesthetic phases of home life."

Radio had graduated from wireless, and the new portable radio "with tubes on flashlight dry cells" made it possible for vacationers to "dance to radio on a mountain top." The notion that radio reception was poor during the summer was earnestly disputed by one *St. Paul Pioneer Press* writer who declared that, "It had actually been found by careful experimentation that on five nights out of six it is possible to obtain results quite comparable with those one enjoys in winter. Of course, during electrical storms, it is not practical to listen in . . ."

When autumn's colors were at their best, motorists could enjoy them by following directions for a short jaunt published in the newspapers. One tour began at East Fourth and Robert streets, crossed the bridge to South St. Paul, and then continued into the country to Inver Grove, Cottage Grove, St. Paul Park, and eventually back to Dayton's Bluff. Motoring, in the adventurous days of the Good Roads movement, was a perilous undertaking for anyone who did not read the newspapers, particularly in early spring.

"Keep Off the Roads," Highway Commissioner C.M. Babcock warned in an urgent plea to motorists not to attempt any trips unless they were sure of road conditions. Babcock added, with a note of gloom, "Road conditions right now are probably worse than they have been any time since the

A Ramsey County Courthouse under construction in
   1931. The tower of the old courthouse, built in 1884
   at Fourth and Wabasha, can be seen at the right. It
   was torn down in 1933.
B F. Scott and Zelda Fitzgerald at Dellwood, White
   Bear Lake, a month before their daughter's birth in
   1921.

A

B

automobile came into general use." Fall rains had soaked the roads. Unpaved, often mere double ruts, they promptly froze in the chill of winter and by spring were quagmires.

The state's constitution was amended to permit the borrowing of money to build roads. Congress already had passed the Federal Highway Act which appropriated money for state and county highways, a move that drastically altered American life. The trucking industry was challenging the railroads and propelling St. Paul's Midway District into the fourth largest trucking center in the country.

Horse-drawn vehicles had long been nosing into towns the railroads did not reach and, after the invention of the gasoline-powered vehicle, it was but a short leap for American ingenuity to hook the wagons to the backs of the new horseless carriages. Thus the truck was born. At the beginning of World War I, some 300,000 trucks were operating over such roads as the country had; by the end of the war, a million trucks were in operation.

119

A

A *Moonshiners arrested by federal agents on a farm near St. Paul. Federal agents, according to the Dispatch's account, "ran into two veritable Amazons when they attempted to confiscate a still on a farm near St. Paul." Jailed overnight, the women were released on probation.*

B *Confiscated liquor outside the Old Federal Courts Building where Andrew Volstead and the Northwest Dry Enforcement District had offices.*

120

. . ran into two veritable Amazons . . . to confiscate a still . . .

Any new, faster, more flexible way of hauling goods, including contraband liquor, would have played a role in the failure of Prohibition, called an experiment "noble in intent" by President Herbert Hoover. Indeed, the truck and the automobile were boons to the organized crime of the Prohibition era. Those realists who had predicted that the public simply would not accept the outlawing of liquor had been entirely correct. The 1920s were not years of reform. Rather, this was a period of rebelliousness, often typified for St. Paul, particularly, by F. Scott Fitzgerald. Fitzgerald's work was markedly influenced by his early years here, although he actually spent little more than seven years in St.

Paul. A number of sites are associated with him: the house at 481 Laurel where he was born in 1896; the Summit Terrace row house at 599 Summit Avenue, now a National Historical Landmark where, during the summer of 1919, he rewrote *This Side of Paradise;* the Commodore Hotel, and the University Club where he lived periodically.

The lawlessness and corruption of the bootleg era affected everyone. Half the people in the country, it was said, were making "home brew." Grocers were astonished at the quantities of sugar and raisins they were selling. Mash was cooked in attics, basements, garages, barns, warehouses — anywhere grain, sugar, and yeast could be mixed, fermented,

B

A

and run through a still. Sometimes the stills
overheated and exploded, creating spectacular fires.
"Bathtub gin" was an exotic product of medicinal
alcohol diluted and flavored with gin, bourbon, or
scotch, and then bottled. But the crude liquor
ordinary folk made could not fill the demand.

The more enterprising among the suppliers of
illegal booze smuggled it across the border from
Canada. The profits were substantial, the risks not
great, since the police tended to look the other way
and, if they did not, sentences were light.

Hundreds of speakeasies were located all over the
city, some of them downtown where they did a
thriving noon-hour business. Gambling and
prostitution flourished in the Seven Corners
neighborhood, and along Jackson and
St. Peter streets.

In her book on St. Paul's Old Federal Courts
Building, *A Landmark Reclaimed*, Eileen Michels

describes the constant stream of Prohibition
violators that flowed through the building, and how
the halls were lined with weeping families of men
sentenced to the standard year-and-a-day for liquor
violations. At the opening session of the federal
district court in June of 1923, almost 100 bootleggers
were arraigned. At the same time a federal grand
jury indicted six men for conspiracy to defeat the
Volstead Act by selling bootleg liquor at a soft drink
bar at 346 Cedar Street.

Andrew John Volstead, the man whose name is
associated with Prohibition, had his office in St.
Paul's Old Federal Courts Building. A Granite Falls
lawyer, he was Republican representative to
Congress from Minnesota's Seventh Congressional
District from 1903 to 1922. Volstead drafted and
introduced the Eighteenth Amendment and
sponsored the 1919 legislation that closed down
saloons all over America. Defeated for re-election in

B

C

A *Federal agents investigating a substantial*
     bootlegging operation, 1922.
B *Federal agents breaking up an illegal still, 1925.*
C *Andrew Volstead in 1925.*

A

1922, he moved to St. Paul as legal advisor to the chief of the Northwest Dry Enforcement District. Its offices spread out over most of the building's fourth floor during the height of the government's attempts to enforce the law.

As a young woman, Helen Warren Pfleger worked in Volstead's office with Walter F. Rhinow, a former Minnesota National Guard officer and director of the office, and Mel Harney, assistant director, widely known as an "untouchable." Mrs. Pfleger's work had an old-world flavor:

"General Rhinow occasionally asked me to work at the switchboard at night," she recalled. "He always asked me to call my mother so she would not be worried, and he also had one of the agents take me home in his car. Whenever he asked me to work at night, I knew it was a sign that Harney or his agents were going to make an investigation of some illegal activity and General Rhinow wanted to keep in touch with them by telephone . . .

"Sometimes the agents wore old clothes when they went on assignments in poorer neighborhoods, or when they acted as tramps in order not to be recognized. It was quite a contrast to see the usually well-dressed agents all ragged and down at the heels . . .

"There was a flower shop in St. Paul which was suspected as being a source of illegal liquor . . . . A small flower stand held a display of ferns. The . . . agent looked around the shop . . . and was just about to leave when he happened to notice an extra spigot in back of the flower stand. He turned the

B

B

A *The Hollyhocks on the Mississippi River Drive north of West Seventh Street.*
B *Alvin Karpis in 1936 as "Public Enemy Number One," and in 1970, on parole in Montreal after thirty-three years in prison.*
C *Alvin Karpis on his way to the Old Federal Courts Building where he pleaded not guilty to the kidnapping of William Hamm, Jr.*

C

faucet and out flowed a stream of high-grade intoxicating liquor."

By 1925 it was abundantly clear to police and federal agents that crime syndicates had moved into the illicit liquor trade. Violence was all too common. On April 25, 1927, newspapers headlined three murders committed virtually in the shadow of the State Capitol. The *St. Paul Dispatch* reported:

"Three men are under arrest in the investigation of the triple murder early Sunday of two men and a woman believed by police to have been brutally slain in the third outbreak of gang warfare in the Twin Cities within two weeks."

One of the victims, a woman, was identified as a proprietor of a "drinking place" and the wife of a man shot to death on West Seventh Street four years earlier; the second victim had been acquitted of murdering a man outside the Produce State Bank at Tenth and Jackson during a holdup, and the third

victim, a former hotel bellhop, apparently was in the liquor business.

In 1933 and 1934 federal and state liquor laws were repealed. St. Paul was vociferously divided on the issue. Twenty-four clubs demanded that a balky legislature repeal the state laws, while St. Paul drys, hastily mobilizing their forces, bombarded the state senate with thirty-one petitions. One resolution declared:

"We, the members of the congregation of Dayton Avenue Presbyterian Church, assembled in worship of Almighty God, heartily indorse the action of the members of the Senate in refusing to repeal the enforcement act of our state; and we pray you will stand strong and firm against all efforts to flood our beloved land again with intoxicating liquor so destructive of the physical, moral and spiritual welfare of our people."

Unfortunately, flooding of the land with liquor

A

A *Re-enactment of the Bremer kidnapping of 1934. St. Paul banker Edward Bremer was seized by the Barker-Karpis gang at Goodrich and Lexington avenues as he was driving to work.*

B *Kate (Ma) Barker.*

C *John Dillinger, J. Edgar Hoover's first Public Enemy Number One.*

B

C

A

B

had been immediate back in 1919. Crime had bred upon crime until the physical safety of the people was threatened by organized crime's stranglehold on the city, particularly from 1925 to 1935, a dark decade that was not St. Paul's finest hour.

In 1924 an arrangement was made by the police that was known as the O'Connor System. It was devised by St. Paul's chief of police, John J. O'Connor, who spread the word through the underworld that its members would not be molested in St. Paul as long as they did not commit any crimes there. A self-serving accommodation, it ignored the danger to people elsewhere in return for assurances that St. Paul's citizens would be safe, but it had the support of the city's administration and civic leaders. When Howard Kahn, crusading editor of the *St. Paul Daily News,* spoke out against the system, he was accused of "sensationalism."

The result was predictable. The city was infested with gangsters who rented the best houses and apartments, bought expensive clothes in the best stores, drank the best booze, and outfitted themselves with guns and fast new cars. They partied in the best restaurants, night clubs, road houses, and gambling joints. The late Nate Bomberg, a police reporter for the *St. Paul Daily News* and, later, for the *St. Paul Pioneer Press,* described this period in a chapter he contributed to Eileen Michels' *A Landmark Reclaimed* and in a special Sunday section for the *Pioneer Press* of December 3, 1967.

A favorite gathering place, Bomberg recalled, was the Green Lantern, a bar and supper club at 545-1/2 Wabasha Street. Another was the Hollyhocks on the Mississippi River Drive, north of West Seventh Street, housed in a spacious three-story dwelling with a veranda around all four sides. An exclusive eating and gambling spot that attracted the well-to-do from all over the Twin Cities, the Hollyhocks was plush — formal dress, black tie for men and evening dresses for women. Customers often arrived in chauffeur-driven cars.

There were other notorious night clubs: the Green Dragon Restaurant at Snelling and University

C

A *H. E. Warren, public safety commissioner in 1934.*
B *Frank B. Kellogg, Secretary of State and author of the Kellogg-Briand peace pact.*
C *Pierce Butler, associate justice of the United States Supreme Court.*

avenues, the Boulevards of Paris at Lexington and University, the Brown Derby at Seven Corners, the Plantation at White Bear Lake, and the Hollywood Club at the east end of the Mendota bridge.

Alvin Karpis, top man in the Barker-Karpis gang, particularly liked the Green Lantern and he described it in a memoir, written in 1971, that reflected St. Paul night life during the 1930s:

"It was like a perpetual party. But the greatest blowout was on New Year's Eve, 1932 . . . . There was probably never before as complete a gathering of criminals in one room in the United States as there was in the Green Lantern that night. There were escapees from every major U.S. Penitentiary. I was dazzled."

After Prohibition was repealed, illicit profits from bootlegging dwindled and the gangs increasingly turned to bank robbery and kidnapping. They terrorized cities and communities in the Midwest. The Barker-Karpis gang was one of two of the best-known gangs to seek sanctuary in St. Paul. Its nominal head was Kate (Ma) Barker and it included Karpis, Arthur (Doc) and Fred Barker, and Ma's paramour, Arthur Dunlop, who later was murdered.

Even more important and more menacing was the gang headed by John Dillinger, J. Edgar Hoover's first Public Enemy Number One. With Dillinger during the months he spent in St. Paul were his chief lieutenant, John Hamilton; his moll, Evelyn Frechette; Homer Van Meter; Eddie Green; Tommy Carrol; and Lester Gillis, better known as Baby Face Nelson.

It was inevitable that the O'Connor System would break down. On August 30, 1933, Swift and Company's $30,000 payroll was seized in South St. Paul. One policeman was killed, another injured, and buildings for two blocks around were sprayed with machine gun bullets.

The most spectacular crimes were the kidnappings. Haskell Bohn, son of Gerhard Bohn, founder of Bohn Refrigeration Company in the St. Paul Midway District, was kidnapped. Political boss Leon Gleckman also was seized outside his suite at

The city was infested with gangsters . . .

A

the St. Paul Hotel. In both cases the ransom was paid.

On June 15, 1933, Barker-Karpis gang members kidnapped St. Paul brewer William Hamm, Jr., at the corner of Greenbrier and Minnehaha and forced him into the back seat of a car. He was driven to a house in Bensenville, Illinois, and held for four days while his family frantically rounded up the $100,000 ransom. It was paid and Hamm was released unharmed near Wyoming, Minnesota.

Officials believed that the Touhy gang, led by Roger Touhy, were the kidnappers, even though some members already were in jail in Milwaukee. Their trial in a packed, heavily guarded courtroom in St. Paul's Old Federal Courts Building in November, 1933, attracted national attention as the first trial after passage of the Lindbergh Law. It was also anti-climactic. The suspects were acquitted for lack of evidence.

On January 7, 1934, Edward Bremer, a St. Paul banker, was seized by the Barker-Karpis gang at Goodrich and Lexington avenues as he was driving to work. He also was driven to Bensenville and held in the same house as Hamm. This time, Ma Barker, with a finely developed sense of greed, doubled the ransom to $200,000. Again it was paid and Bremer was set free near the West End Commercial Club. Little of the ransom money was recovered. The scanty information available suggests that it was laundered through the racetracks in Cuba.

A *Line-up, during the 1920s.*
B *Slot-machine raid in St. Paul in 1935. Widespread gambling was part of the organized crime of the Prohibition era.*

B

A *A newspaper cartoonist's commentary on the
   "O'Connor System." Devised by St. Paul's Chief of
   Police, John J. O'Connor, it had the support of civic
   leaders William Hamm and Otto Bremer. It is an
   irony of history that one legacy of the system was
   the kidnapping of a Hamm and a Bremer.*

B *Household aid by women working under a WPA
   program.*

Now, however, reaction set in. St. Paul's wealthy families, most vulnerable to kidnappings, were in a state of panic. No one felt safe. They appealed for help to Washington where a number of St. Paul men occupied positions of distinction. Frank B. Kellogg, author of the Kellogg-Briand peace pact, was secretary of state; Pierce Butler was associate justice of the supreme court, and William Mitchell was solicitor general. Homer Cummings, United States attorney general, called St. Paul a "hotbed of crime, poison spot of the nation, a haven for criminals, a citadel of crime." Newspaper editorials attacked St. Paul as "a protected city" that invited "scores of big-time crooks to make St. Paul their hangout." They labeled the situation "a disgrace" and a "shame before the whole country." Howard Kahn called for reform in a series of front page editorials in the *Daily News.*

Finally an investigation began. A blue ribbon Ramsey County grand jury was empaneled to probe charges of laxity in law enforcement. It released its report on March 31, 1934. Resolutely looking the other way, it declared, incredibly, that there was "no justification for any charges that an excess of crime exists here."

With exquisite timing, that same day John Dillinger and his mob shot their way out of an apartment at Lincoln and Lexington avenues. St. Paul detective Henry Cummings and a federal agent had answered a call concerning "suspicious people" and had been greeted by gunfire when they knocked on the apartment door. Dillinger escaped with the rest of the gang, including Evelyn Frechette, a rather quiet, ordinary young woman of French-Canadian ancestry whose only mistake seems to have been falling in love with Dillinger.

B

A

The morning of the shoot-out, St. Paul's mayor, William Mahoney, issued a political pamphlet claiming that the kidnappings had been "fake kidnappings concocted by the press." Mahoney was locked into a hot mayoral election with his challenger, Mark H. Gehan, a contest distinguished by a near riot at Selby and Snelling avenues when 2,000 people tried to get into Liberty Hall, which seated 250, for a Mahoney-Gehan debate.

The campaign forced Mahoney into making ridiculous charges. He claimed that Cummings' statement had been instigated by the Northern States Power Company, that "St. Paul has no more gangsters than any other city" and that "if there are any gangsters here it is because they have been invited by the newspapers. They (the newspapers) have assured gangsters of protection in St. Paul." Gehan won by a narrow margin.

H.E. Warren, a reform candidate, became public safety commissioner in 1934 and orders went out to clean up St. Paul. On the theory that gangsters should not be able to out-gun the police, the newspapers started a fund to buy better guns for the force. The shoot-out at Dillinger's apartment had been an eye-opener. Police found the gangsters had "more up-to-date fighting equipment . . . than is possessed by the entire St. Paul police force," according to news reports. The police department, it seems, possessed only one machine-gun, one tear gas gun, and one bullet-proof vest, and that had been confiscated from a gangster.

Warren was succeeded by Gus Barfuss, a no-holds-barred law enforcement officer. Slot machines were picked up, gambling joints and houses of prostitution closed down, liquor licenses revoked, and dishonest cops dropped from the force.

B

A *Protest group at State Capitol, sometime during the early 1930s. One of the signs reads, "Use all the ROTC funds for needy students."*
B *WPA pay demonstration, November, 1935. The police were called out to maintain order as WPA workers sought a pay increase.*
C *Guardsmen mobilizing at the Minnesota State Fairgrounds during the Truck Drivers' strike in Minneapolis in 1934. St. Paul drivers did not join the strike but 600 St. Paul National Guardsmen were among 3,500 called to duty when Governor Floyd Olson declared martial law.*

C

Sixth Street, looking east from Wabasha, about 1920.

The F.B.I. spread a net for Dillinger, and shot and killed him in Chicago. A month later, Homer Van Meter was shot down by St. Paul police near University Avenue and Marion Street. The F.B.I. captured Alvin Karpis in New Orleans in May, 1936. His trial in St. Paul's Old Federal Courts Building was heavily guarded by two dozen agents armed with submachine guns. Karpis wore leg irons as well as handcuffs when he was moved from the Ramsey County jail to the detention room on the second floor of the courts building.

Convicted and sentenced to a long prison term, he also was indicted later for the Bremer kidnapping. Evelyn Frechette was tried in the Old Federal Courts Building, and went to prison for harboring Dillinger. Most of the other outlaws went to prison or died violently.

A dark and tragic decade had come to an end. The country at large was trying to recover from the Depression set off by the stock market crash of 1929. Part of the untrammeled exuberance of the 1920s had been channeled into stock speculation. These were prosperous years, with good wages, high prices, and plenty of jobs. Industry produced, people bought durables, the public invested in stocks, and everyone expected good times to last forever. But production finally outran sales, factories cut back, workers were laid off, and the value of stocks, inflated during the speculative get-rich-quick years, began to fade. In October of 1929, the market crashed. On October 24, the Associated Press reported from New York:

"The remarkable era of avid public speculation in stocks which has swept over the country during the past five years came to a climax today in the most terrifying stampede of selling — totaling 12,894,680

A

B

shares — ever experienced on the New York Stock Exchange and other leading security markets . . . Not since the war panic which resulted in closing the exchange for seventeen weeks in 1914 has Wall Street seen such a dark and trying day and never in financial history have security markets been thrown into such a tumult."

In St. Paul, brokerage offices were crowded until after dark for the first time in history. Standing room was at a premium. The ticker tape ran four hours late and lights burned far into the night as clerks worked overtime to get their books ready for the opening of the market the next day.

The Depression was the worst in the history of the country. Twelve to fifteen million people lost their jobs and millions, without money to pay taxes and interest on mortgages, lost their homes. Agriculture already was in bad shape. Farmers had expanded

A *The only transportation available after a snow storm on March 29, 1924.*
B *Christmas in St. Paul, 1927.*

Minnesota's fabled snowstorms . . .

A

A *Water tower dripping ice during one of Minnesota's fabled snowstorms.*
B *Aftermath of a snowstorm — February 8, 1936.*

B

production to feed a Europe and an America at war between 1914 and 1920, but throughout the 1920s exports and income fell off sharply. Thousands of rural banks closed and entire villages went bankrupt.

Thus, Recovery was really the only issue during the 1932 presidential campaign. Franklin Delano Roosevelt spoke in the new St. Paul auditorium on April 18, 1932, to a crowd of 7,500 men and women, the largest dinner gathering ever held in the Northwest, according to newspaper coverage of his speech. He demanded that the "power interests" either cut the electric rates or that the federal government step in to control electric power productions, and he called for help for farmers and small merchants through "greater consumption" by way of "more factory wheels turning and more employment."

In March, 1933, 20,000 farmers crowded into St. Paul to plead with state legislators for tax relief and aid for debtors. Clad in overalls, they jammed the Capitol's corridors and galleries and massed on its front steps while their spokesmen appeared before a three-hour joint session of the senate and house. They demanded moratoriums on mortgages and evictions, taxes on oleomargarine and chain stores, abolition of deficiency judgments, limitation of mortgage interest to not more than one-third the gross receipts of a farm, retention of the Rural Credit Bureau, a state banking system, and increased taxes on utilities. And they threatened reprisals if their demands were not met. Governor Floyd B. Olson joined the demonstrators on the Capitol steps. He charged that "reactionary Conservatives" in the state senate were holding up "constructive relief legislation."

In St. Paul, officials were struggling with the city's own problems. They proposed daylight saving time so that people, who were more dependent than ever before on their vegetable gardens, would have

A Downtown St. Paul from south of the Wabasha
   Street bridge, about 1921.
B St. Paul's skyline in 1927. The old State Capitol at
   Tenth and Wabasha can be seen at right center.

A

B

more time to work in them. And they revived a plan that St. Paul had pioneered forty years earlier during the Depression of 1893. Then a Citizens Committee for the Relief of the Unemployed, including representatives from the Chamber of Commerce and the Trades and Labor Assembly, offered jobs rather than charity to destitute workers. Men were put to work on city streets and parks at wages of $1 a day. Certain laborers were paid instead in firewood and groceries.

In 1933 the Mayor's Work Emergency Committee mounted a campaign to put money into circulation and provide jobs. Money was pledged by individuals and by business and industrial firms so out-of-work men could be hired to make property improvements. Committee members canvassed the city by wards, scrounging money from residents and businesses. Newspapers ran "Give a Job" pledges for people to fill out and mail in. As of March 1, 1933, more than $400,000 had been pledged. The campaign attracted

national attention. J.L. Shiely, campaign vice chairman, was invited to New York to explain the plan, and Chicago officials came to St. Paul to find out for themselves.

Because of the need for job programs that would stimulate business, construction projects were launched that made radical changes in St. Paul. Old buildings were torn down, new ones were built, highways were rerouted, and bridges were constructed under Public Works Administration (PWA) and Work Progress Administration (WPA) programs.

Probably the most dramatic change began in 1927 with city financing, but it was completed under PWA. Buildings on the south side of Third Street from Hill Street to Robert were torn out and the street widened into Kellogg Boulevard, named for Frank B. Kellogg, former Secretary of State.

At Third and Jackson, work got under way in 1932 on a new post office. It was erected on the site of the

old Union Depot which had been replaced by the
new colonnaded Union Depot, completed in 1923.

As the Depression deepened and people struggled
to keep up their courage, parades supporting
Roosevelt's New Deal and particularly the NRA
(National Recovery Administration), became part of
the common experience of these years. In August,
1933, 40,000 people, led by the city's chief business,
financial, and industrial leaders, marched through
downtown St. Paul in an NRA parade organized by
the St. Paul Junior Association, and ending with a
mass rally in Rice Park.

Under the various recovery programs, major
repairs were made on St. Paul's schools, libraries,
parks, and playgrounds. Most of the streets in the
downtown districts were re-paved; West Seventh
Street was widened; a sewer system for Como Park
was built; Holman Municipal Airport was

144

. . . if a general war begins, "we shall inevitably be drawn into it . . ."

resurfaced; a nine-foot channel was constructed in the Mississippi River, and a retaining wall was built along the Lower Landing. In a massive improvement project at the Minnesota State fairgrounds, the old wooden sections of the grandstand were replaced by a modern concrete structure, the grounds were landscaped, and a parking lot created.

In the early 1930s, the present city-county courthouse at Wabasha and Kellogg Boulevard was built and the old castle-like city hall, erected in 1884 on "courthouse square," between Fourth and Fifth and Wabasha and Cedar, came down.

People began to worry about traffic hazards. In 1933 St. Paul's City Council considered an ordinance setting a 35-mile-an-hour speed limit on arterial streets. The Kiwanis Club formed 3,000 St. Paul residents into a Citizens Vigilance Committee. They reported speeders and other traffic violators "in a concerted effort to stop the unnecessary sacrifice of human lives."

Round trip railroad tickets at forty-per-cent-off were offered visitors to the 1933 Minnesota State Fair and the Northwest Livestock Exposition. That year the fair presented the Disappearing Water Ballet, "an elaborate production in which water nymphs performed intricate ballet steps around a sylvan pool."

Less cultured entertainment was endured by residents living around Lake Phalen who protested against "immorality, obscenity and drunkenness" at the Phalen beach. They presented a petition to Mayor Mahoney, charging that "obscene auto-bathing parties" at all hours of the night attracted loafers, hoodlums, and thieves, with the result that "property values have depreciated 20 to 30 per cent because of objectionable conditions." The aroused citizens demanded vigilant police supervision and recommended that a second beach be established at the north end of the lake "where there are no residents to suffer disturbance."

St. Paul alleys — dirt lanes in the 1930s — were passable if spread with a coating of cinders during muddy spring break-ups, and, in a new service to customers, automobile drivers could buy their tires at gas stations.

St. Paul housewives were urged to consider the convenience and safety of mechanical refrigeration in keeping milk, meat, and fresh vegetables fit for the table. And a unit type of air conditioner designed for the home was introduced in St. Paul.

In 1939 Mrs. Franklin Delano Roosevelt opened the first evening program of the Women's Institute of St. Paul, a meeting in the arena of the St. Paul auditorium attended by 12,000 women, more than 5,000 of them from out of town.

People reading the St. Paul papers that summer of 1939 might have noticed a small news story out of Washington, quoting Nicholas Murray Butler, president of New York's Columbia University, as predicting that, if a general war begins, "we shall inevitably be drawn into it . . ."

Help us
CONSERVE
for
DEFENSE
NOW
This STATION OPEN
7 AM to 7 PM
PURE
PURE

Part Five/Rebirth: The Post-War Renaissance

On September 1, 1939, Germany invaded Poland and on September 3, Great Britain and France declared war on Germany and World War II began.

Not for a year would events in Europe have much of an effect on life in St. Paul but, after the fall of France in 1940, Congress passed the Selective Service Act and the drafting of men began.

Armistice Day of 1940 will never be forgotten by anyone in Minnesota who lived through it, but not because it was a reminder of the war to end all wars. It was the day the worst November blizzard in the history of the Northwest blocked every main road in the state and tied up St. Paul for two days. Thousands who had been at work when the storm hit at mid-morning found automobile and streetcar traffic at a standstill when they tried to get home

Gas rationing, daylight-saving time — both part of the war effort's need for conservation.

that night. Hotels were filled and the YMCA and YWCA rounded up cots and established emergency dormitories.

An estimated 2,000 cars were stalled downtown in rush hour traffic and, as late as 10 p.m., at least forty trolleys were stopped all over the city. One of the worst tie-ups was at the Selby Avenue bridge near Hamline Avenue where twenty streetcars were stalled on slippery rails.

The storm, which was early in the season even for Minnesota, caught the city unprepared. Only a few snowplows were ready for service, so Public Works Commissioner Milton Rosen had mechanics mount snow plows on oilers, flushers, and other heavy equipment used in street maintenance. He also assigned fifteen crews to spread cinders on the city's hills. Throughout the Northwest, scores of communities were isolated, as winds whipped snow into huge drifts, and there were at least thirty-four known dead.

That same November, more than a year before the attack on Pearl Harbor, a cautious call-up of reserves began. The 18th Infantry Battalion, a Marine Reserve ground unit activated at St. Paul in

147

A

B

148

C

1939, was sent to Camp Elliott, California, and then to Iceland. Later it fought in the South Pacific. St. Paul's 206th Infantry Regiment became part of the 101st Anti-aircraft Brigade assigned to coastal defenses. Navy and Marine Air Reserve squadrons began training at Wold-Chamberlain Field where buildings to house the men mushroomed all over the base and the sky was filled with open cockpit biplanes, called "the yellow perils."

On nine separate occasions, Minnesota's National Guard units were alerted, creating confusion in the lives of many men who closed their offices, resigned from jobs, or dropped out of school. Finally, on February 10, 1941, they began to report to their stations. As part of the 34th "Red Bull" Division, they were sent to Camp Claiborne, Louisiana, for training. Still under construction, the camp was a miserable place. The grounds were covered with ankle-deep mud and the men shivered in the ceaseless rains and raw, penetrating winds.

All Naval Reserve units were ordered to active duty, including a group of St. Paul men who belonged to the 47th Naval Reserve Division of the 11th Battalion. They were assigned to an over-age

THE WHITE HOUSE
WASHINGTON

January 4, 1943

Dear Mr. Ridder:

The President has learned with much
satisfaction that, in keeping with the war
spirit, the St. Paul Winter Carnival Association
has discontinued its annual event and instead
is staging a great patriotic demonstration to
exemplify St. Paul's part in the war.

The purpose of this pageant of
patriotism, with its emphasis on more and more
production in all war tasks, is most laudable.
The President hopes the entire presentation will
be an outstanding success and that it will inspire all who participate with a renewed appre-
ciation of the eternal values which are at stake
in the war to preserve the Four Freedoms.

The President has much pleasure in
sending hearty greetings to the entire community.

Very sincerely yours,

STEPHEN EARLY
Secretary to the President

Mr. Bernard H. Ridder,
St. Paul Winter Carnival Association,
St. Paul, Minnesota.

A

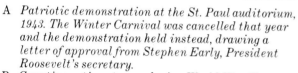

A *Patriotic demonstration at the St. Paul auditorium,
1943. The Winter Carnival was cancelled that year
and the demonstration held instead, drawing a
letter of approval from Stephen Early, President
Roosevelt's secretary.*
B *Counting ration stamps during World War II.*
C *Actress Marlene Dietrich with Sergeant Leonard A.
Richards of St. Paul, after a USO show somewhere in
the war zone.*

destroyer, the *U.S.S. Ward* and on December 7, 1941,
the *Ward* was on patrol off the entrance to Pearl
Harbor.

About 6 a.m., shortly before the first wave of
Japanese dive-bombers rounded Diamond Head, the
Ward spotted something in the water and closed in
to investigate. It was a midget submarine trying to
slip through the net guarding the harbor. The *Ward*
opened fire with a four-inch gun mounted on top of
the ship's deck house, hit the conning tower and
sank a two-man submarine the Japanese had
launched as part of the attack.

The *Ward* had fired the first American shot of
World War II. When the ship's armament was
changed several months later, the gun was removed
and preserved. The *Ward* itself was sunk in the
battle for the Philippines near the end of the war.
During the Minnesota Statehood Centennial in 1958,

the gun was brought to St. Paul and mounted on the
Capitol grounds as a monument to the state's
fighting men of World War II.

The morning after the Pearl Harbor attack, and
for days thereafter, long lines of young men formed
at the Old Federal Courts Building where the armed
services had recruiting offices. Fort Snelling was
activated as an induction center, and business and
industry swung into war production.

The hysteria of World War I was notably absent.
No one suggested a Minnesota Commission of Public
Safety, even though the possibility of sabotage was
in everyone's mind when the Ford Motor Company
plant began to manufacture armored vehicles and
the army, to protect the plant, asked that
Mississippi River Boulevard be closed off. At the
same time, the Minnesota Aeronautics Commission
restricted flights out of three airports around the
New Brighton small arms plant. St. Paul's war
plants manufactured an array of materiel from
wooden gliders to submarine nets.

A bomber modification center was opened at
Holman Field, where more than 5,000 employees
engineered and installed special equipment on

A

military planes that were flown in from all over the country. Many of the pilots used to ferry the planes were women. Among the equipment installed were gunsights developed by Norman B. Mears of St. Paul. Another St. Paul man, Robert Morris Page, director of the United States Navy Research Laboratory, developed and built the first pulse radar in the world.

Prices, wages, and salaries were frozen, and the rationing of sugar, meats, butter, canned goods, fuel oil, gasoline, even shoes, began. St. Paul's Consolidated War Price and Ration Board opened its offices at 53 East Sixth Street and issued books

with ration stamps to each person in a family — blue stamps for canned goods and red stamps for meats and butter. College students surrendered their ration books to their dormitories or rooming houses and it was considered good form for house guests to contribute ration stamps to a host's household. Automobile drivers displayed "A," "B," or "C" gas ration stickers, and just so everyone could keep their coupons straight, the St. Paul newspapers published weekly ration calendars.

St. Paul restaurant owners complained to the Office of Price Administration that rationing was ruining business, that they could not get enough

A   *Victory Garden fruits and vegetables proudly
    displayed in 1944.*
B   *Toy-lending program for youngsters, 1944.*

B

food to serve the increasing number of customers
who were eating out to supplement their own
rationed food at home. They established "meatless"
days with menus that featured non-rationed
chicken, turkey, and fish — a plan that spread to
households and launched a blizzard of recipes for
vegetable dishes. Some of those vegetables came
from Victory Gardens that blossomed in front yards,
back yards, and vacant lots all over the city.
Industrial firms also planted gardens and St. Paul's
Victory Garden Council awarded prizes each season
for the best gardens.

An additional 300 streetcars were put into service
in St. Paul to handle extra rush-hour riders created
by gas rationing. Rubber for tires was in critically
short supply. To save both tires and gas, newspapers
advised readers to drive only when absolutely
necessary, keep tires properly inflated, have them
inspected regularly, observe the thirty-five-mile-an-
hour speed limit, and share cars with others. Thus
the car-pool was born.

The fear of air raids was particularly acute after
the Japanese bombed Dutch Harbor in the Aleutians
in the spring of 1942. "If enemy bombers were
reported soaring toward St. Paul tonight," the
Pioneer Press asked its readers, "how well prepared

153

A

would they find the city for such an attack?" St. Paul and other major Midwest cities were told to anticipate "token raids," and Civil Defense officials in Omaha warned that the Twin Cities were particularly vulnerable "because they have war industries and are transportation centers."

Air raid wardens were appointed to patrol sections of the city. The Home Guard, policemen and firemen and their auxiliaries, doctors, nurses, Red Cross workers, Boy Scouts, were trained in civil defense. Air raid shelters were set up. In the event of an attack, St. Paul officials pointed out proudly, 14,000 trained persons could be called out in the city. Air raid warden command schools were held in Stem Hall of the city auditorium, with 500 staff officers attending at a time.

Lights in downtown store windows and on theater marquees, cafes, and night clubs were turned down in a "brown-out" to save energy and make the city less visible from the air. A group of civilian boat-

B

A   *A golf match with Bing Crosby and Bob Hope at Midland Hills Golf Course May 18, 1942. Proceeds went to Army-Navy Relief.*
B   *V-E Day Celebration — Minnesota Federal Savings and Loan building.*
C   *Victory in Europe, May 8, 1945. Newsboy Dale Zimmerman calls his "Extra!"*

C

A

A *The old Lower Landing during the 1940s.*
B *Downtown St. Paul between 1940 and 1959. Much of the old city of the late 19th century was still intact.*

owners was organized into the Coast Guard Temporary Reserve. Using government picket boats and their own craft, they maintained a twenty-four-hour patrol around dams and bridges on the Mississippi, the St. Croix, and the Minnesota rivers.

For the first time in more than ten years, newspapers were full of help-wanted ads. The War Manpower Commission office at 55 East Fifth Street advertised for men to build an airfield in Nebraska, transportation paid, two to three months of work, seventy hours a week, and time-and-a-half over forty hours. Men between 35 and 55, "no experience necessary," were sought as warehouse men, truckers, receiving clerks, retail clothing salesmen — the list was endless.

Women were recruited for jobs that once went to men only. They replaced men on the assembly lines of St. Paul war plants and essential industries. So many women were working night shifts, as well as days, that the YWCA organized swing shift dances that began at 1 a.m.

Other aspects of women's lives were changing. As

Lois P. Hatton, the *Pioneer Press'* fashion editor, wrote: "Wartime conditions have made it necessary for many women to undertake washing and ironing who never before attempted this work, and the art of ironing — and it is a fine art — has baffled many a beginner." Mrs. Hatton then carefully described how to iron rayon fabrics, a real problem, as many women who lived through the experience vividly recall. They also remember the thick, heavy rayon stockings that took two days to dry and sometimes split into runs on the first wearing.

There was a decided push in St. Paul for enlistments in the Women's Army Corps and a board was set up to interview applicants. More than 500 women applied and were sent to Fort Snelling for physicals. Other St. Paul women worked at the British War Relief headquarters at 501 Grand Avenue, repairing and reconditioning clothing to be sent to bombed areas in the British Isles. Eleanor Roosevelt visited the St. Paul headquarters in April, 1943.

There were the lighter moments. Louis

B

157

A

"Satchmo" Armstrong, "the trumpet king of swing," played a one-night stand at the Prom Ballroom on University Avenue in 1942. Radio stations — the first one established in St. Paul by Stanley E. Hubbard, founder of one of the first broadcasting systems in the country — brought listeners the Burns and Allen show, the Kate Smith hour, the March of Time, Dinah Shore, Kay Kyser, newscaster Cedric Adams, and such commentators as Dr. Harold Deutsch, Major George Fielding Eliot, Raymond Clapper, and Gabriel Heatter.

St. Paul's movie theaters showed either escapist films — "Life with Father" (Percy Waran), "The Pride of the Yankees" (Gary Cooper, Theresa Wright, Babe Ruth), "Hello, Frisco, Hello" (Alice Faye, John Payne, Jack Oakie), "Road to Morocco" (Bing Crosby, Bob Hope, Dorothy Lamour), or war movies — "Commandos Strike at Dawn" (Tim Holt, Bonita Granville), and "Day of the Avengers," plus special war department films, such as "At the Front," a documentary on the fighting in North Africa.

As the end of the war approached, the state was caught up in a typically heated controversy launched by its traditionally rambunctious legislature. The furor was over daylight saving time, instituted at the beginning of the war and ended by the legislature in 1945, after heart-rending representations by rural legislators that daylight saving time played hob with farm work.

A *Korean War veterans at a Christmas reunion in 1951. A lighter aspect of the new war, this reunion brought together friends who had attended St. Paul's grade schools and high schools together before joining the marines. Left to right are Sergeant James Fredericksen, Bill Williams, and Bob and Dick Fletcher.*
B *Korean War veterans at St. Paul's Union Depot. Red Cross volunteers met the men as they were on their way home on May 9, 1951, for a thirty-day leave.*

B

A *Led by Mitchell Baron, left, and Joe Schnotze, co-chairmen, the Minnesota Volunteers, Kennedy for President caravan leaves St. Paul to take part in Kennedy's Wisconsin campaign.*

B *A common scene in offices throughout St. Paul as news of President Kennedy's assassination November 22, 1963, reached St. Paul on television.*

A

B

As a result, St. Paul, Minneapolis, and 170 other cities in the state stayed on "war time" — daylight saving — while rural districts switched over to standard time. The confusion in St. Paul, where state offices were forced onto standard time in a city operating an hour ahead of them, was immense. It was repeated in the early 1960s when the same clash of wills over the same matter produced similar results.

With the end of the war, the thousands of new families the war had created faced a housing shortage that was acute. Newspapers reflected this in their want ads:

"$100 Reward.

Ex-Navy Lieut. & wife want to rent 1 or 2 bedrm. furn. apt. or duplex."

"Responsible couple & baby girl desire furn. or unfurn. apt. Excellent ref. Will paint or decorate if needed."

"39 Coupe, beautiful cond. Will sell for rental of house or apt."

The need for housing was coupled with the need for transportation. Sometimes an exchange was proposed:

"Midway District — Modern apt. in exchange for new car."

"Five Room Apt. and bath for delivery of new automobile."

St. Paul's population had been growing even during the war years. Between December, 1941, and

A *Rain-drenched marchers entering Central High*
   School April 7, 1968, for a tribute to the Reverend
   Martin Luther King.
B *Memorial march in tribute to Martin Luther King,*
   April 5, 1968.

A

B

June, 1942, the city's population increased by 7,500
to 297,781, despite the large number of men who had
left for military service, according to figures
assembled by the Economic Stabilization Research
Institute of the University of Minnesota. It was the
largest rate of growth in a half century,
including World War I, and demonstrated the
impact of war production on the city.

The post-war chaotic population explosion into
the suburbs was a vast movement created by a
variety of factors: new buying power by people who
had accumulated savings during the war years when
there was little to buy; Depression-era survivors
who were longing for their own homes after the
doubling-up of families that had been necessary
during the years of privation, and the formation of
thousands of new households by returning veterans
whose dreams of a home of their own had

sustained them and the women who waited for
them. Real estate developers bought up farm
acreage and woodland in Ramsey County, divided it
into precise squares, and set small, neat little
houses in the middle of each square. The first of
these houses seldom had more than 1,000 square feet
of living space, but they were the American dream
for young couples who painted and papered their
mortgaged castles while their children played on
dirt yards.

Suburban populations doubled and quadrupled:
Roseville increased from 4,650 in 1940 to 23,997 in
1960; South St. Paul from 11,884 in 1940 to 22,032 in
1960; North St. Paul from 4,248 in 1950 to 8,520 in
1960; Arden Hills from 916 in 1950 to 3,930 in 1960.
With this growth came streets, gas lines, water,
schools, and shopping centers for a populace that
had, in a few short years, transformed the

A

A   *Selma protest rally, Unity Church, March 11, 1965.
     Senator (now vice president) Walter Mondale
     stands, at left, with the Reverend Kenneth Beck of
     St. Cloud, and the Reverend Leon Gladish of House
     of Hope Presbyterian Church, St. Paul.*
B   *NAACP members march on the Capitol.*

recreational automobile into a necessity.

The effect on St. Paul was stunning. The enormous population shift left behind an aging city, a disproportionate number of families who could not afford the suburbs, and a downtown whose customers were shopping elsewhere. Urban renewal seemed a solution to the core city's problems. As an urban renewal brochure pointed out, ''We have not been fixing up our cities as fast as they have been wearing out!'' Of 93,359 dwelling units surveyed in St. Paul in the late 1940s, 3,792 were dilapidated, 13,607 did not have private baths, 13,310 did not have central heating, and 10,361 had more than one person per room. From one-third to one-half of St. Paul's people lived in neighborhoods showing these serious signs of blight.

Urban renewal started in the late 1940s with clearance in the Capitol Approach area, the culmination of an effort that had begun in 1903 when Cass Gilbert completed the Capitol. Gilbert presented a Capitol Approach plan for widening Cedar Street and placing federal, state, and municipal buildings on each side of the street. The plan and variations of it were periodically examined

B

Construction of the new Federal Courts Building at
Kellogg Boulevard and Robert Street in 1966. A
much-needed boost to downtown renewal, the
building anchored the first section of the city's
remarkable skyway system.

...2,641 people were homeless...Damage...in the millions...

and ignored or rejected, although some attempt at symmetry was achieved when the Minnesota Historical Society building, completed in 1916, and the State Office Building were placed on either side of the Capitol.

With the end of World War II, city and state officials took a good look at the neighborhood around the Capitol. One of the oldest sections of the city, it was crowded with tenements, boarding houses, lean-tos, second-hand stores, rubbish piles, and billboards. Capitol improvement plans were tied in with construction of the Veterans Service Building as a war memorial. As part of the project, guided by the Governor's War Memorial Advisory Committee working with a $2 million legislative appropriation, the dilapidated buildings in the area were torn down.

Urban renewal programs elsewhere in St. Paul began in 1949 with passage of the Federal Urban Renewal Law. The state legislature already had approved creation of the Housing and Redevelopment Authority of the City of St. Paul. Within the next decade, under HRA and the St. Paul Port Authority, authorized to develop land along the river, many homes and business structures dating from the 19th century and located in blighted areas were razed. New housing developments were built, beginning with the John J. McDonough Homes at Jackson and Arlington, and the Franklin D. Roosevelt Homes at Maryland and Hazelwood.

One neighborhood at which the Port Authority took a hard look was the Upper Levee, a residential district on the river flats at the old Upper Landing. The idea for a riverside parkway running through the area had been discussed since 1889 when the City Council acquired some of the earliest right-of-way. In the early 1950s, plans were maturing,

although industrial needs dictated a road that bore little resemblance to a parkway. Funding for what became Shepard Road was approved by the voters in 1953.

A year earlier, the greatest flood in Minnesota history poured into the lowlands of the St. Paul area. From Fort Snelling to Inver Grove, such huge sections as the Upper Levee, Lilydale, and Holman Field were isolated, and 2,641 people were homeless. Damage was in the millions of dollars. The river crested on April 16, 1952, at 22.2 feet, eight-and-a-half feet above flood stage and two-and-a-half feet above the previous all-time high set in 1881. (Another major flood in 1965 nearly destroyed the Riverside development, the industrial area along the flats that replaced some of the oldest buildings on the West Side.)

Renewal work had been curtailed during the Korean War which broke out in June, 1950. The 47th, or Viking, Division of the National Guard, made up almost entirely of Minnesota men, was called into service and sent to Camp Rucker, Alabama. The Air National Guard, including the 109th squadron from St. Paul, also was mobilized and assigned to bases within the United States.

The great fear during the Korean War centered around atomic bombing. Asking, "How Safe are You if St. Paul is Bombed?" the *St. Paul Dispatch* announced a series of articles that would carry survival instructions from scientists, military experts, and civil defense officials who had studied the effects of atomic bombing. After almost two years of service, both the Air National Guard and the Viking Division returned home in December, 1953.

The planning for urban renewal went on, despite the new war. A major problem downtown after

...fifty-six new buildings have been completed...

World War II was the increasing number of autos crowding the streets. Between 1921 and 1940, streetcar traffic decreased 57 per cent, while automobile traffic increased 481 per cent. Clearly, something had to be done. Buses had been used for mass transit as early as 1921 and now conversion from streetcars, which took up the center of the narrow streets, to buses began in earnest. After the last streetcar run was made in St. Paul on October 31, 1953, one-way streets were designated in the downtown district.

Before the end of World War II, the federal government had developed a plan that had a profound effect on St. Paul and other cities throughout the country. This was the 1944 proposal of the National Inter-regional Highways Committee for an interstate highway system to link cities with populations of more than 300,000. The proposed interstate for St. Paul, however, forced a change in a plan for downtown renewal which had been developed in 1958, when St. Paul businessmen commissioned a proposal from the Victor Gruen firm. The state highway department decided to route Interstate Highway 94 south instead of north of the Capitol, and the Gruen plan had to be abandoned. Other ideas surfaced, proposed by HRA and the City Planning Department, and supported by the St. Paul Chamber of Commerce and the Metropolitan Improvement Committee, a group of labor leaders and professional and business people who had organized to promote commercial renewal throughout the city.

In a twelve-block area in downtown St. Paul, outdated office buildings, most of them built before 1920 and few remodeled since the 1930s, were hard-pressed to find paying tenants. The public complained that stores lacked desirable merchandise and services.

Even more serious, "the decline of the downtown business district seriously eroded the city's tax base," wrote Mary Davis, in the December 19, 1974, issue of *The Downtowner.* "An unfair burden fell upon the residential districts when the downtown area was no longer able to pull its weight."

MIC's — the private sector's — answer to the problem was the Capital Centre Renewal Project which was approved in 1962 by the City Planning Board and administered by the St. Paul Housing and Redevelopment Authority. The project was funded by a $19 million grant from the federal government, with the city paying the remaining $6 million, plus administrative costs. More than 100 buildings spread over forty-three acres in the heart of downtown were involved in the project. Most of the old buildings were torn down, despite some anguished cries from historic preservationists who tried to save a number of fine old structures. (Historic preservation in downtown St. Paul blossomed later with the successful effort to preserve and restore the Old Federal Courts Building and the McColl Building, both of them on the fringes of the Capital Centre.)

A commitment by the federal government in 1961 to build the new Federal Courts Building in downtown St. Paul helped renewal along. Construction of the Civic Center and the municipal parking ramp at the west end of the downtown district was also part of the planning for the city. Another potent factor in downtown renewal was the construction of the Hilton Hotel, now the Radisson.

As of mid-1977, fifty-six new buildings have been completed in downtown St. Paul, with estimated construction costs of $279,542,000. The new structures represent an interesting mix: retail stores in one cluster, commercial and business firms in another, and residential building in still another

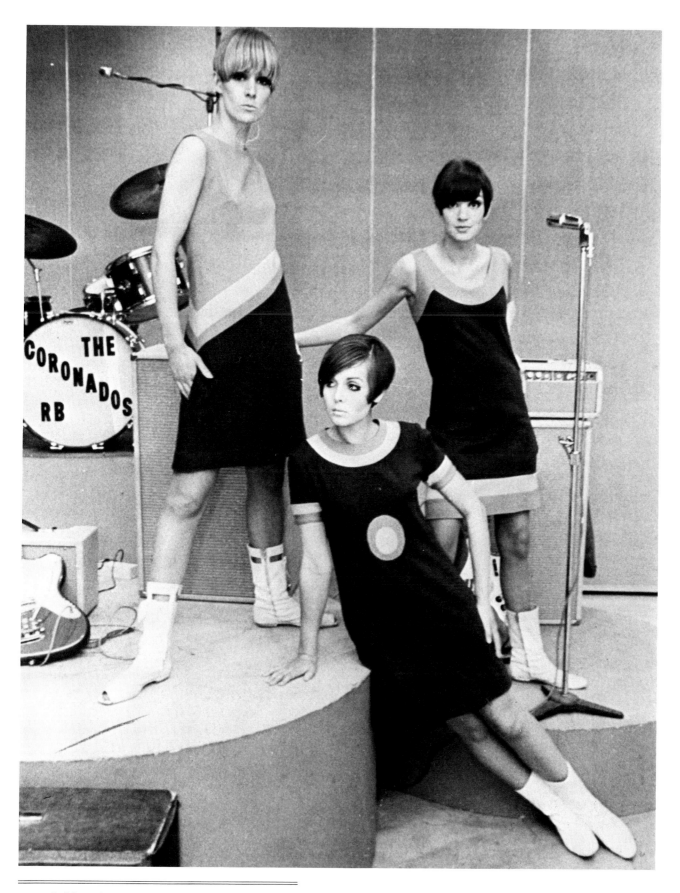

1960s fashions, inspired by London's Mary Quant, on display in St. Paul.

A Marchers approaching Selby Avenue from Summit
during a 1960s peace march.
B Pickets from the Minnesota Peace Action Coalition
demonstrating against the Vietnam War at St.
Paul's federal building.

— Kellogg Square Apartments overlooking the Mississippi. Another ten buildings are being built or renovated, with construction costs of $136,850,000, and twelve more buildings are proposed, with further construction costs estimated at $253,000,000.

A remarkable skyway system links the buildings in and around Capital Centre, in a system that is studied by planners from all over the world. The first public skyway in the Twin Cities, and one of the earliest in the country, was built in 1966 between the new Federal Courts Building at Kellogg and Robert Street and the Pioneer and Endicott buildings across Fourth Street. Eight more skyways were added between 1968 and 1974, and six more are planned through 1979.

The downtown's innovative business leaders now are working on a decades-old plan for developing Seventh Street into a tree-shaded mall with benches, fountains, and bus lanes. A projected people-mover system is part of the plan.

One of St. Paul's favorite armchair occupations, however, is analyzing itself and redevelopment still presents some problems seeking solutions. "Block A" at Seventh and Cedar, is still a gaping hole accommodating, as a temporary solution, a parking lot. Restauranteurs, hotel men, and theater-owners fuss about lack of after-five activity, but St. Paul people traditionally dine at home at night, despite the earlier gaudy night life in the 1920s and 1930s.

The city has been called the "Boston of the West." In its social and cultural institutions, the city does reflect some Yankee influence, stemming, perhaps, from some of its early leaders who were New Englanders, but its German settlers also strongly influenced the cultural life of the city. The zeal with which early St. Paul organizations

A *Pro and anti-Israeli factions outside St. Thomas
   College just before a 1975 rally for Israel.*
B *An Ad Hoc Freedom Committee demonstrating at a
   meeting in St. Paul of the Minnesota Citizens
   Concerned for Life.*

established libraries was one manifestation of an urge toward uplift. It may be no accident that there are nine colleges and universities in St. Paul, a phenomenon that reflects the role of the churches, since most of the colleges grew out of the city's major religious institutions.

Macalester College is the oldest higher education institution with a continuous existence in St. Paul. It was founded in 1854 by the Reverend Edward Duffield Neill as the Baldwin School, on the site later occupied by the Old Federal Courts Building. Neill moved the college to St. Anthony, and then back to St. Paul, to its present site at Snelling and Grand avenues, where it opened in 1885.

Hamline University at Hewitt and North Snelling avenues originally was established in Red Wing, also in 1854, but the Panic of 1873 forced the school to close. It was moved to St. Paul where it reopened in 1880.

The city has three Roman Catholic colleges: St. Thomas College at Summit and Cleveland avenues, founded in 1885 by Archbishop John Ireland; the College of St. Catherine at 2004 Randolph Avenue, established in 1905 as a preparatory boarding school and college for women; and the St. Paul Seminary at 2200 Grand Avenue, founded in 1894 to train men for the priesthood.

Bethel College, now at 3900 Bethel Drive, Roseville, was founded in 1871 at Como and Snelling as a seminary for the Baptist General Conference in America. Later a junior college, it became a four-year liberal arts college for men and women in 1947.

Concordia College, at Syndicate and St. Anthony avenues, is a Missouri Synod Lutheran college established in 1893 as a high school on the site of the state's old reform school. Luther Theological Seminary at 2375 Como Avenue, founded in 1879, is the largest Lutheran seminary in America.

William Mitchell College of Law, 875 Summit Avenue, an evening law school for men and women that numbers Chief Justice Warren Burger among its graduates, was originally the St. Paul College of Law and dates from 1900. In 1956 it was renamed for William Mitchell, associate justice of the Minnesota Supreme Court from 1881 to 1899, and represents a series of mergers with other Twin Cities law colleges.

The University of Minnesota's St. Paul campus began life as the State Agricultural College founded in 1868 on a tract of land east of the Minneapolis campus. By 1887 the present site in St. Anthony Park had been acquired and the first building erected.

The city's cultural heritage is suggested by the nationality groups that have put their stamp on the city. The Germans and the Irish are the most visible, by weight of numbers, influence, or both. The first person of German ancestry to settle in St. Paul was Jacob W. Bass, who was born in Braintree, Massachusetts, in 1815, arrived in St. Paul in the 1840s, served as postmaster between 1849 and 1853, and ran the St. Paul House, an early hotel. The 1880s were the peak years of German immigration. They settled in the Fifth Ward, around Assumption Church in downtown St. Paul, and in the Eighth Ward, around St. Agnes Church in Frogtown. They attended church services in German, and read one of a number of German-language newspapers. The first such newspaper in St. Paul was the *Volks Zeitung,* founded in 1855. The Germans brought with them a love of music and they founded musical groups that were the forerunners of St. Paul's present major musical organizations. For many years, the city's German quarters were filled with saloons, signboards in German, and German-language social clubs and schools.

How the Irish, in the persons of three soldiers from Fort Snelling, first settled in St. Paul, already has been described. By the 1850s, the Irish had begun to arrive in force. In 1857, according to one newspaper account, St. Paul's police force consisted of nine Irishmen and one "American." John Ireland, who was born in Ireland and who became

174

A

A   *St. Paul, looking downstream from the High Bridge, with Harriet Island on the right.*
B   *The gun from the U.S.S. Ward on the Capitol grounds. Manned by St. Paul Navy Reservists, this was the gun that fired America's first shot of World War II.*

B

A

A *Osborn Building, Capital Centre.*
B *Capital Centre reflections. The Osborn Building in the center is reflected in the Northern Federal Building at the left. Both buildings are part of the city's magnificent Capital Centre renewal project. The St. Paul Athletic Club's early 1920s building is at right, with the First National Bank building behind it.*

B

FOLLOWING PAGE OVERLEAF
The lights of St. Paul, from Dayton's Bluff.

St. Paul's first archbishop, arrived in 1852. With
James J. Hill, he colonized railroad land with his
countrymen who followed him to work on the
railroads. The Irish traditionally have dominated St.
Paul's politics, but they are most highly visible
during their riotous St. Patrick's Day parade each
March. The first celebration of St. Patrick's Day in
St. Paul was described in the March 20, 1851, edition
of the *Pioneer:*

"The Sons of the Emerald Isle, and our citizens
generally, joined in an impromptu celebration of the
anniversary of St. Patrick, on Monday last. The
Stars and Stripes were elevated to the peak of the
liberty pole in front of the Central House; but
unfortunately, the wind being high, the tall mast
was broken off, some twenty feet from the ground.
The flag was then raised upon the stump and a
salute fired. Speeches were then made.

"It was proposed that the celebration be
continued by a supper at Barney Rogers . . . . After
supper was over, a procession was formed, headed by
a band of music & numbered some three hundred,
which marched through the principal streets,
visiting the residences of many of our citizens."

The exuberant parade apparently got out of hand
some years later. Archbishop Ireland himself
inveighed against what he called the "midnight
orgies," and the parade ceased to be held. Revived in
1967 after more than fifty years, the parade takes
over the city each March 17 as Irish, part Irish, and
synthetic Irish drink green-colored beer in a day-
long spree.

One of the largest immigrant groups in St. Paul
during the 19th century was the Canadians but,
except for the few who spoke French, they have been
so inconspicuous that history has overlooked them.

Archbishop Ireland himself inveighed against . . . the "midnight orgies". . .

James J. Hill was born in Canada and did not become an American citizen until 1880. As investors in Hill's enterprises and other St. Paul firms, Canadian citizens have had a considerable impact on St. Paul's business community, a trend that is still seen today.

The first Jews arrived in St. Paul early in the 1850s. In 1857 they chartered Mount Zion, the city's first Hebrew congregation, and in 1871 they built their synagogue at Tenth and Minnesota streets. During the 1880s, a large number of Jews who had fled from Russia settled in West St. Paul and in the Mt. Airy district east of the present Capitol. As they prospered, they moved near the Cathedral where they built the Reformed Temple Mount Zion and the Conservative Temple Aaron. Others settled in Highland Park.

A few blocks beyond Seven Corners on West Seventh Street is the old immigrant community of Czechs, Slovaks, and Moravians. Czech Hall, still standing today, was an important social center for the community.

St. Stanislaus Church on Western Avenue and Superior is the center of the city's Polish community founded by the Polish families who settled around the Upper Landing and built houses on piles driven into the marshy ground. About 1880 Italian immigrants joined the Poles on the levee and created the colorful community known as "Little Italy." Construction of Shepard Road forced them to move.

The Scandinavians settled on the east side of St. Paul where they worked as craftsmen, and built hundreds of homes in St. Paul. Like the Germans, they organized many singing societies. Mexican or Chicano neighborhoods emerged on St. Paul's West Side when the earlier Jewish families moved across

The site of old downtown St. Paul where the permanent settlement of the city began. In April of 1839, Edward Phelan and John Hays, natives of Ireland and discharged soldiers from Fort Snelling, established claims to the land now covered by Shepard Road and running along the river from the center to the right of this photograph. In May of 1839 Pierre "Pig's Eye" Parrant took up a claim just east of Phelan and Hays. He built his whiskey shanty on a rise of land about where Shepard Road runs under the Robert Street bridge in the center of the picture. The present post office on the left stands on the site of the old Union Depot which, in turn, was built on the site of the St. Paul and Pacific Railroad's little depot.

A

B

the river. The Mexican workers had been brought in to help in the sugar beet fields of western Minnesota and some of them migrated to South St. Paul to work in the packing plants. There also are small settlements of American Indians on the West Side, in Frogtown, and on Payne Avenue where the American Indian Center is located.

In St. Paul's North End a Romanian community has settled down, and there is also a cluster of Syrian and Lebanese families.

The city's black community can trace its heritage to James Thompson, who was at Fort Snelling in 1827, then settled at Kaposia, where, since he spoke Sioux, he served as interpreter for the Reverend Alfred Brunson, the first Methodist missionary in the St. Paul area. Thompson later moved to St. Paul and helped build some of the first

residences in the city.

After the Civil War, blacks came to St. Paul to work on the railroads and to establish small businesses. They settled primarily in the Selby-Dale area, but there also was a settlement in South St. Paul by blacks who had been meatpackers in Chicago and had moved to South St. Paul when branch packing plants opened there.

For almost all of St. Paul's ethnic groups, the strong cultural differences of the early years have softened with time and assimilation into the community, but each group keeps its heritage alive through its traditional festivals. The cultural mix is most clearly seen in the programs of the International Institute, founded in 1919 as a YWCA program to aid young women of foreign birth. Every three years the Institute holds its Festival of

182

C

A Swans gliding on Lake Como.
B Farmers' Market at Tenth and Jackson, a favorite with early Saturday morning shoppers during the growing season.
C "Above, Above," Alexander Liberman's massive red metal sculpture in the Garden Plaza of the Osborn Building, Fifth and Cedar streets.
D The Conservatory at Como Park, built in 1914 and 1915.

D

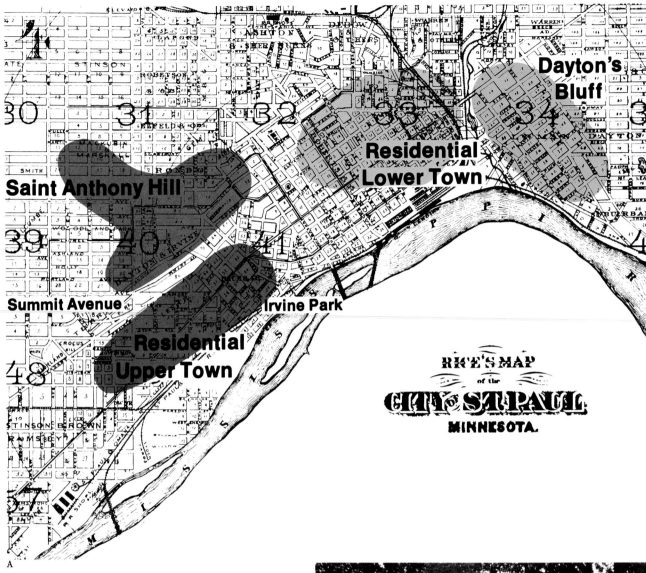

Dayton's Bluff

Residential Lower Town

Saint Anthony Hill

Summit Avenue

Irvine Park

Residential Upper Town

RICE'S MAP
of the
CITY OF ST. PAUL
MINNESOTA.

A

A *The colored areas show the location of four of*
St. Paul's "inner ring" neighborhoods.
B *Ready for restoration — Ramsey Hill district.*

B

A

A Irvine Park restoration in progress. The first
National Historic District in St. Paul, this once-
elegant residential district is now in the midst of an
exciting renewal that has an interesting history of
its own. This neighborhood is the only one of St.
Paul's first residential districts to survive from the
1850s. However, by the 1960s, the area had
deteriorated so badly that plans were under way to
tear down all the houses and replace them with
apartment buildings. Efforts to preserve and restore
the district were inaugurated by the Ramsey County
Historical Society in 1968 when Society staff and
Board members began a series of meetings with
neighborhood residents and representatives of the
St. Paul Housing and Redevelopment Authority. In
1972 the Society submitted to the Minnesota
Historical Society a nomination of the Irvine Park
district to the National Register of Historic Sites.
With the interest of the state historical society now
enlisted, the historic district was established and
an Irvine Park Special Redevelopment Committee
created to work out a plan for preservation and
restoration of the area. Committee members
included a representative of the Ramsey County
Historical Society, the Minnesota Historical
Society, the St. Paul HRA, the St. Paul City
Planning Department, and the West Seventh Street
Association. In a long series of meetings lasting
throughout 1973, the committee worked out a plan
that would be economically feasible, selected the
initial developer, and designated buyers for each of
the historic houses. The rest is history. The Irvine
Park Historic District, a pioneer in restoration
projects in the Twin Cities area, is one of the most
exciting of these efforts because the houses are the
last survivors of downtown St. Paul's earliest years
and because the district had decayed so badly before
restoration began.

B

B Restoration — the Historic Hill District. This
spacious two-story family home on Laurel Avenue is
typical of many such pre-World War I houses that
now are being restored in the Ramsey Hill district.

A

B

C

D

D   *Summit Terrace at 587-601 Summit Avenue, the row house where F. Scott Fitzgerald lived in 1918 while completing revisions on* This Side of Paradise.

E   *James J. Hill's mansion at 240 Summit Avenue. Built of red sandstone and completed in 1891, at a cost of $200,000, the house has been designated a National Historic Landmark by the National Parks Service.*

A   *The Old Federal Courts Building on Rice Park. Saved from destruction by a group of dedicated preservationists, this old post office and federal courts building is under restoration by Minnesota Landmarks, Inc., as an arts and culture center. It is scheduled to reopen in the summer of 1978 as Landmark Center.*

B   *"Riley Row," also known as Laurel Terrace, one of the row houses in the Ramsey Hill district. Built in 1887, it wraps around the corner at Nina and Laurel Avenue.*

C   *Park Square Court on the north side of Mears — once Smith — Park. Built in 1886 of red pressed brick and sandstone, it housed, first, Noyes Brothers and Cutler Wholesale Drug Company, and later, the B.W. Harris Company, which began business as an early fur company. The building has been restored to house restaurants and small shops.*

E

A

B

C

A *Rarely noticed — the fascinating alleys threading between the older buildings still standing in downtown St. Paul.*

B *Interior of the St. Paul Cathedral, completed in 1915. Its Neo-Baroque decoration is lavish, with stone carvings, metal grille work, imported colored marbles, and a rose window, among its other stained-glass windows.*

C *One link of many in St. Paul's remarkable skyway system, believed to be the most extensive public concourse in the world.*

A

A *The magnificent pipe organ in James J. Hill's Summit Avenue mansion. He filled his two-story art gallery with his Barbizon paintings.*
B *A mural lending color and character to a wall in the West Side's Mexican-American neighborhood.*
C *One-room country school frozen in time for city children. Restored to the 1890s period, this little schoolhouse stands on the grounds of the Ramsey County Historical Society's Gibbs Farm Museum at Cleveland and Larpenteur. Classes are held each summer for youngsters who "go to school" as their great grandparents once did.*

B

C

189

Nations in which different nationality groups present native foods and dances.

By the middle 1960s, construction of the freeway system was approaching completion. Interstate 94 followed a portion of the old ox cart trail that once led from St. Paul to St. Anthony, and 35-E stretched northward, along the western edge of the maze of railroad tracks that followed still another ancient transportation route, the Trout Brook-Phalen Creek waterway. Both freeways changed the configuration of St. Paul — Highway I-94 cut off Rice, Wabasha, and Cedar streets that once stretched from the bluff's edge in downtown St. Paul to Capitol Hill.

The city is still primarily a transportation center.

At the Lower Landing, where steamboats once tied up, barges now unload their freight at municipal terminals along Warner Road. The hauling of freight on the river was revived in 1925 when St. Paul businessmen joined those in other cities to form a barge line. During the 1930s a nine-foot channel was dredged to accommodate barge traffic. Pipelines carrying oil from the south and from Canadian oil fields have made St. Paul a major petroleum distribution point. The first pipeline into Ramsey County was laid in 1931.

Just as St. Paul was an international port of entry in earlier years when steamboats, stagecoach lines, and railroads linked the city with Winnipeg, the

...it is not difficult to imagine what ... old St. Paul looked like.

airlines flying in and out of Minneapolis-St. Paul International Airport have maintained both cities as an international point of entry and departure for overseas.

Air travel and air shipping in the Twin Cities date back to the early 1920s. Regular air mail service began April 20, 1920, with a mail route to Chicago run under the direction of the United States postal department. Its base was a small hangar at Speedway Field, a race track south of Minneapolis that became Wold-Chamberlain Field. Surplus army planes were used in a daily round-trip schedule, but after eight planes and four pilots were lost in nine months, service was discontinued for seven years. In 1926 an air mail contract was secured and the city of St. Paul purchased 230 acres on the West Side for $60,000. A single hangar was built for $17,000, and what is now Holman Field became operational. It was named for Charles W. "Speed" Holman, one of the most colorful figures of the early days of aviation. He earned his nickname as a motorcyle racer before he became a pilot, and he won air races, did stunt flying exhibitions, and established a speed record for a commercial airplane over a commercial route. When he was killed stunting during an Omaha air show on May 17, 1931, 100,000 people attended his burial on Pilot's Knob at Acacia Cemetery. During the 1930s, Holman Field was expanded and today, private and corporate planes use the field.

St. Paul's national impact goes far beyond its traditional role as a transportation and wholesale center. It is the fourth largest printing center in the nation, and headquarters for electronics, computers, chemicals, metal products, sandpaper, paper and wood-processing firms, many of them with 19th century roots but turning out late 20th century products.

An easy blend of the traditional and contemporary helps create a special ambiance that is best caught on a late spring evening if one stands at Wabasha and Kellogg Boulevard, the site of old Bridge Square. The boulevard curves to the west and

north, along the route of the ox carts that lumbered into town from the Northwest. A few blocks away is the Irvine Park Historic District, the last remaining residential section that dates from the 1850s. It is now being restored to the elegance it represented during the last half of the 19th century when Alexander Ramsey lived in his mansion a block from the park.

Running along the bluff above Irvine Park is Summit Avenue, perhaps the most historic and beautiful street in the Midwest, and one of the great streets of America. It is a part of the Ramsey Hill Historic District, whose homes and business structures are being restored in a back-to-the-city movement which is part of the 1970s life-style.

Two blocks north of Bridge Square is the magnificent and stately Old Federal Courts Building, now Landmark Center. Saved from the wrecking ball by interested citizens and civic officials, the building was one of the first two historic structures in the country to be transferred by the federal government to local agencies. In 1974 the Board of Ramsey County Commissioners took over the annual maintenance and operation of the building and Minnesota Landmarks, Inc., a non-profit agency, is restoring the building as a cultural center to house arts and historical agencies.

If one looks east, down the river from the site of Bridge Square, it is not difficult to imagine what the heart of old St. Paul looked like. Bench Street drops off, down the bluff, and a half-block north on Wabasha is the site of the early Opera House. The north side of the boulevard follows the approximate route of Third Street, which was lined on both sides with two- and three-story buildings. The street still slopes gently downhill toward Jackson Street and the Lower Landing, still there but buttressed by concrete.

And if the hour is late and the sun is setting, the light catches the white bluffs that tower above the eastern, downstream curve of the Mississippi, the landmark the early explorers described and the Indians called *Im-in-i-ja Ska.*

191

Part Six/Partners in Growth

T he sinew and bone of any city
are the businesses that provide the jobs
and pay the taxes.
In the following section of this book,
you will learn how many of the leading businesses
and industries were founded, grew and played
their vital roles
in the history of St. Paul.

Brown & Bigelow

It was just a little print shop, one room on the second floor of a neglected downtown building. Smoky kerosene lamps swung from the sooty ceiling. The place reeked with ink and dusty type. Amidst it all, stood 25-year-old Herbert H. Bigelow, fussing with his old printing press. He concentrated on the simple calendar he had just completed. It was enterprising creation, Bigelow thought. A handsome bust of George Washington decorated the calendar alongside the words, "Schleh Brothers — Fuel Dealers."

"Give your customers something useful," young Bigelow told John Schleh, his first customer. "That way, they'll be reminded of you 365 days a year."

"Terrific," Schleh agreed, when he saw the first calendar displaying his company name in commanding type. "I'll take 250."

John Schleh's order put Herbert Bigelow into business on February 7, 1896 — a business that earned $13,000 in the first year and now reports annual sales in the neighborhood of $60 million.

Throughout its history, Brown & Bigelow has been a St. Paul resident. In its first 11 years, the firm outgrew three locations and then settled on a 17-acre site that was once the Lexington race track in the Midway district of St. Paul in 1906.

Never quite satisfied with his product, Herbert Bigelow explored new ways to better his specialty advertising business. Not long before, Bigelow had produced the first color calendar in America and adorned it with a still-life called "Luscious Fruit." Next he expanded his line to include ink blotters — a simple, yet effective way to convey an advertising message, Bigelow reasoned. Soon, Brown & Bigelow was making more ink blotters than the next 10 companies combined. The firm also claimed the largest specialties sewing factory in the world, producing more than 50,000 painters' caps and 6,000 horse covers every day. The arrival of the automobile cut into horse blanket trade, but that shift in consumer interest didn't deter Bigelow. Every item emanating from his plant carried an advertising message for a growing number of St. Paul clients.

Early in the firm's history, Bigelow hired an inventive employee named Charles Ward, who was

A

B

later to become the founder's successor. On the side, this $25-a-week punch press operator invented Brown & Bigelow's first desk-calendar — a design that appealed so much to Harry Truman that the President had one in his White House office.

Ward was responsible for a number of advertising advances, including advertising playing cards introduced by the firm in 1927 and the (Redilite) pen light, a welcomed novelty for American consumers.

In the years approaching World War II, business at Brown & Bigelow was booming. With Herbert Bigelow's death, the aggressive young Ward took over and, during his tenure, many more products were added to the basic Brown & Bigelow calendar line.

To assist in the war effort, Ward was aksed by the United States Under Secretary of War, Robert P. Patterson, to "divert your great calendar business to war work — by turning your production to making War Posters . . ." Patterson counted on Brown & Bigelow's extensive distribution network to rally citizens of this country: "If you can place a war subject where every calendar buyer would normally place a peace time calendar, you could cover the nation effectively,'' Patterson said.

It goes without saying that the patriotic Ward did just that.

Today, Brown & Bigelow is a highly diverse firm, still specializing in advertising specialties. Although the traditional "barbershop'' calendar has been replaced by executive appointment books and decorator-styled calendars for the home, the basic commodity is still a mainstay of Brown & Bigelow business today. In addition, the firm has become a leading manufacturer of playing cards, leather-bound books, moulded plastic desk and household accessories, greeting cards, fine prints, clocks and vinyl personal items. All the company's manufacturing is still carried on at the St. Paul Midway site.

Brown & Bigelow was acquired by Saxon Industries in 1970, a *Fortune* 500 conglomerate based in New York. The St. Paul firm is responsible for approximately 10 percent of Saxon's total business.

C

D

A	Brown and Bigelow's St. Paul Midway plant.
B	Early downtown location
C & D	Two representative examples of turn-of-the-century calendars.

Burlington Northern

No question about it — the king of American inland transportation in the 1850's was the steamboat. The emerging railroad train had little clout. It was, in the minds of many, not much more than a teakettle on wheels pulling a few wooden boxes along a string of spindly iron rails. At best, the railroad train was a support mechanism that simply connected one navigable body of water to another.

In those early years, St. Paul was clearly a river transportation center. Many times each week, passenger and cargo boats steamed into town bringing settlers and essential goods. St. Paul was the Western frontier (to many Easterners, in fact, it was considered the end of civilization).

Local business visionaries could see, however, that river transport was not to be the end-all. Minnesota and territories beyond had millions of uncharted, resourceful acres. Some method had to be devised to move products of that land to transportation centers. With that, the railroad era dawned and the flames of enterprise were fanned by people like James J. Hill, Henry Villard and J.P. Morgan.

The stories of countless railroad enterprises are interwoven with the history of St. Paul. In fact, at one time there were at least nine separate railroads serving the city. The business was highly competitive and railroad owners jealously guarded their empires. Some railroads suffered serious financial problems and were engulfed by their more successful rivals. Many merger attempts were made as years passed, but one of the most significant did not occur until 1970, when the 25,000-mile Burlington Northern system, based in St. Paul, was formed through the combination of four companies — the Chicago, Burlington & Quincy, the Great Northern, the Northern Pacific, and the Spokane, Portland and Seattle railways. That merger represented more than 15 years of discussion, planning and legal effort. With the merger, the new Burlington Northern network serves 19 states and two Canadian provinces.

It all began on June 28, 1862, when the St. Paul & Pacific Railroad (forerunner of the Great Northern) began offering the first rail passenger service in St. Paul. That service amounted to only a ten-mile stretch of track connecting St. Paul and the landlocked village of St. Anthony. The service was established by a consortium of St. Paul businessmen who realized that passengers and goods had to find their way to thriving St. Anthony (now a part of

A

B

Minneapolis). James J. Hill acquired the railroad in 1878 and set in motion ambitious expansion to the Far West. By 1893, Hill had completed a transcontinental link connecting Seattle, Washington, and the East.

Just two years after St. Paul & Pacific originated its St. Anthony service, President Abraham Lincoln signed an Act of Congress giving another railroad — Northern Pacific — the authority to build a line between Lake Superior and Puget Sound. Ground was broken for the main Northern Pacific line just west of Duluth in 1870.

Construction began in the West at the same time. In little more than a decade, Northern Pacific crews from East and West met at Gold Creek, Montana, September 8, 1883, to drive the last spike. That event established Northern Pacific as the first of the northern transcontinental railroads and President Henry Villard, a German immigrant, was credited with completion of that tough project.

In the early 1900's, the Great Northern and Northern Pacific — dominant railways of St. Paul at the time — acquired The Burlington Railroad, an enterprise operating mainly in Illinois, Wisconsin, Iowa, Missouri, Nebraska, Colorado and Wyoming. In the same decade, the two railroad giants also created the Spokane, Portland and Seattle railway system as a joint enterprise designed to provide northern lines to Oregon.

Although Great Northern and Northern Pacific cooperated on both ventures, they were serious rivals, so it took years to arrive at the 1970 merger plan.

Today's Burlington Northern Inc. is still headquartered in downtown St. Paul in what is considered America's most spacious railroad headquarters building. Approximately 3,100 employees work in that building. The corporation is involved in many facets of the transportation business, including truck, airfreight and rail, and in the natural resources business — timber, manufacturing and sale of forest products, and development and management of oil, gas, coal, iron ore, taconite and other mineral resources. The corporation is also involved in land and real estate management. Burlington Northern Inc. now has expanded to include more than two dozen subsidiary companies. Annual revenues for the huge firm that had its beginning with "teakettles on wheels" in 1862 now approaches $2 billion.

C

E

F

D

A *James J. Hill*
B *Henry Villard*
C *St. Paul & Pacific's* Wm. Crooks, *first locomotive in Minnesota.*
D *Northern Pacific's first locomotive,* the Minnetonka
E *L.W. Menk, chairman and chief executive officer, Burlington Northern Inc.*
F *N.M. Lorentzsen, president, Burlington Northern Inc.*

Cardiac Pacemakers, Inc.

Although they didn't start business at the turn-of-the-century, as many St. Paul companies did, the founders of Cardiac Pacemakers, Inc. (CPI), were truly pioneers when they incorporated in 1971. Four men — two engineers, a marketing specialist and a salesman — decided to invest their future in a new theory for heart pacemakers developed by researcher Wilson Greatbatch. Greatbatch had discovered a new lithium power source for pacemakers that was sure to eclipse the conventional mercury-zinc cell used in the earliest models. But Greatbatch couldn't sell his idea to the handful of pacemaker manufacturers already doing business in 1971. Too risky, some said. The conversion to lithium is too expensive, others argued. So Greatbatch appealed to the four men who knew the pacemaker industry well, but didn't have a business of their own.

With that, CPI was off and running with $200,000 and a small, one-story production facility on North Cleveland Avenue in St. Paul. Since Pacemaker production requires some of the cleanest, highly refined assembly conditions possible, the firm, at first, could produce only one pacemaker a week . . . a stainless steel and plastic unit weighing about 165 grams. Since that time, however, the firm has produced approximately 35,000 pacemakers for patients of all ages all over the world. Mrs. Johanna Roever, 80, of Cedarburg, Wisconsin, was the first human recipient of a CPI pacemaker powered with the lithium-iodine battery in 1972. Another early patient was 16-year-old Duluth resident, Paul Robinson, who is, today, an electronics technician at CPI's new headquarters in Arden Hills, a suburb of St. Paul.

Since the firm introduced its lithium-powered pacemaker, every major pacemaker manufacturer in the United States has developed a similar unit. The lithium battery has proven to be a more effective power source than mercury zinc because it has a longer life, it is solid state, it is predictable and it can be completely sealed off from body fluids. The original 165-gram pacemaker of five years ago has now been reduced in size and weight by more than 50 percent — today's "MINILITH"® pacemaker produced by CPI is no larger than a cigarette lighter. Even smaller models are being developed.

Most pacemakers are implanted with a local anesthetic and positioned just below the collarbone.

Although CPI has not been in business long enough to qualify as "historic" in the same way one might look at many other St. Paul firms, CPI is certainly historic because of its pioneering in this specialized field.

A&B   *Cardiac Pacemakers, Inc., attractive new
        headquarters in Arden Hills*

B

Central Warehouse Co.

St. Paul, Minn. April 21, 1902

Geographically speaking, the Midway area of St. Paul was the best by far. It was an ideal distribution point for many business firms of the early 1900s and continues so today because of its central location to St. Paul and Minneapolis. People used to call the Midway area "The Third City," and even James J. Hill, the undisputed Empire Builder of Minnesota, built a railway to serve the area.

Little wonder that C.P. Bratnober of Waterloo, Iowa, picked the Midway area to start a commercial warehouse business. He was drawn to St. Paul because of his interests in the sale and distribution of lumber and the increasing importance of this commodity to the economy of Minnesota. Surely, industrial and commercial activity spawned by lumbering and other new enterprises would spark a healthy need for storage space. Thus, Central Warehouse was founded by C.P. Bratnober in 1902, and was the first company to provide storage and public warehousing services in St. Paul. Land O'Lakes Creamery began its early warehousing activities at Central along with Hancock Nelson Mercantile Company and the Hershey Chocolate Corporation.

By 1916, Central recognized a need for additional rail service to its warehouses and surrounding industries. In response to this need, Bratnober purchased a locomotive from the historic Dan Patch railroad line and set an important business precedent. As years passed, railroad transportation became more and more important until nearly 10,000 cars a year carried goods to and from industries in the area over the Central Warehouse Railroad.

Today, the warehousing business has changed dramatically. Rail transportation has given way to truck. Central's operation has grown from 40,000 square feet of building area to 750,000 square feet, and from seven acres of land to 27 acres. The firm stores and distributes general merchandise and perishable products for its clients throughout a six-state area. Central Warehouse also offers refrigerated warehousing, freight consolidation, computerized inventory control, trucking and leased warehousing. Since the firm's beginning, however, some important factors have stayed the same — the original Midway site has changed only through expansion and modernization, ownership of the business is still controlled by the Bratnober family and Central Warehouse still operates its own railroad.

Electric locomotives owned by the Central Warehouse Co. give prompt switching service over four miles of private trackage.

Sixteen modern trucks of Central's fleet are available for instant local delivery to points in the Twin Cities and vicinity.

199

Dayton's

A

B

Although Minnesota's leading retailer didn't become a part of St. Paul history until 1958, the dramatic business agreement that brought Dayton's department store to the city made up for lost time. In a well-attended news conference on November 28, 1958, Donald Dayton, president of the 56-year-old Minneapolis store, and Carl Schuneman, Sr., president of the 70-year-old St. Paul retailing institution, announced a merger. Shoppers in St. Paul suddenly had the best of both cities wrapped up in the new Dayton's-Schuneman's department store at Sixth and Wabasha. What's more, the five Dayton brothers and their cousin, George, also announced the purchase of an entire city block in St. Paul. That block — bounded by Cedar, Wabasha, Sixth and Seventh streets — was to become a $7 million, five-floor, 633,000-square-foot retailing complex just five years later.

From the beginning, the Dayton enterprise seemed destined to grow. George Draper Dayton, a Worthington, Minnesota, banker, opened his investment company on Nicollet Avenue in Minneapolis in 1901. In hopes of attracting tenants for his building, George backed two young men in a dry goods store on the site. When their operation failed one year later, George and his son discovered they had a store on their hands. Within 25 years, however, the small retail establishment called Dayton's was transformed into one of the leading department stores in the country.

Today, Dayton Hudson Corporation is a diverse retail enterprise with properties including department stores (46 major facilities in Minnesota, North Dakota, Michigan, Ohio, Arizona, Nevada, Oregon, and Oklahoma), covered shopping centers, low-margin stores (60 in 10 states), and specialized retail outlets handling books, jewelry, and electronics. Compared with other major retailers nationwide, Dayton Hudson ranks 19th in total sales

and 11th in net income, according to a 1977 *Fortune* Magazine survey. Total annual sales for Dayton Hudson now approach $2 billion. The firm is also extensively involved in real estate development and management.

Dayton's involvement in downtown St. Paul has been particularly significant. A 1958 newspaper editorial said the Dayton-Schuneman merger represented a "new era for St. Paul" and lauded the Dayton brothers for selecting one of the older blocks in the downtown area to redevelop. Since then, the Dayton management has been an important force in planning for the city's entire redevelopment district.

C

A   *Dayton's acquired Schuneman's in January, 1959. The store, which then became known as Dayton's St. Paul, was located at Sixth and Wabasha.*

B   *Dayton's built a new downtown St. Paul store in 1963, on a site bounded by East Seventh, East Sixth, Wabasha and Cedar — the first store of its kind to integrate shopping and parking.*

C   *The street was blocked off on the day Dayton's moved from the Schuneman's building into the new store across the street.*

Degree of Honor Protective Association

The liberated woman was alive and well and doing a respectable business in St. Paul decades ago. In fact, St. Paulites like Frances Buell Olson and Edna Dugan had a corner on the market when they helped originate the Degree of Honor Fraternal insurance organization expressly for women in 1910. The aim of that new enterprise was a sound one: no woman, if she could help it, wanted her death to be a financial burden on the family. But beyond such a concern, women of the early 1900's saw little value in personal insurance, even when they were lucky enough to afford it. The average policy written in those days was worth $500. In addition, no woman was permitted to buy more than $1,000 worth, a fact that Edna Dugan, now 81, reluctantly accepted. Mrs. Dugan, a long-time officer of the Degree of Honor Protective Association, bought her $1,000 whole life policy in 1914 and still has it.

Along with basic insurance, the Degree of Honor nurtured social ties and service projects for St. Paul women in the early years. St. Paul women hopped streetcars and rode as long as an hour to attend their Degree of Honor lodge meetings. There was loyalty and a rare sense of fun in the ranks. Nearly every St. Paul neighborhood had its own lodge.

All along, Degree of Honor members have had an eye on civic involvement. They planned regular visits to the St. Paul Crippled Children's Home; they made cancer pads for countless hospital patients; and when there was a death in a member's family, her sisters rallied in every way they could.

Today, members of St. Paul's Degree of Honor lodges carry on many of the same civic activities. Many lodges now meet, however, in the white granite, ten-story tower that members built in 1961 in downtown St. Paul. There have been other notable changes, too. In 1924, men were admitted as members in the fraternal insurance association, and a Junior Department for young boys and girls was established. Today, a total of 84,000 are Degree of Honor policyholders. Even though men now constitute about half of the adult policyholders, women still have an edge, Edna Dugan adds with elfin enthusiasm: "Women's rates are still cheaper . . . and we continue to outlive those dear men."

The total membership in the Twin City area is 5,218.

A

B

C

D

E

A & B   (Left) The new and (right) the old
    C   Frances Buell, first National President
D & E   (Left) 1961 dedication and (right) Glee Club

Donovan Companies, Inc.

A   B

C

D

George Donovan was an energetic, young apprentice in the construction business long before he started his own company in St. Paul nearly 60 years ago. As a young man, George traveled into the rural areas of Minnesota supervising installation of telephone lines for AT&T. He learned about surveying, managing men and equipment, and dealing with proprietary farmers.

By age 30, George Donovan was ready to start his own business. He pulled together enough people and machines to take on small, electric power-line jobs around Minnesota and, steadily, the Donovan Companies grew to be one of the largest electrical

construction contractors in North America. Total company revenues now hover around $150 million annually and approximately 1,000 people draw Donovan paychecks.

George Donovan has been joined by his three sons, Richard, John and Gerald. Together, the four long-time St. Paul residents run Donovan Companies, Inc.

Donovan family enterprise and creative risk-taking wove a colorful history for the firm. Fascinated by the new prospect of supplying natural gas to homes and businesses in the 1930's, for example, George Donovan convinced the city farmers of Bath, New York, that he could provide all the natural gas the modest community needed. Donovan built 20 miles of pipeline to serve Bath and still holds the town's natural gas contract. Bath customers have now been joined by nearly 50,000 more in Florida, Wisconsin, Minnesota and Iowa. Total cubic feet of natural gas sold by Donovan approaches 32 billion annually. In addition, Donovan's propane business now totals more than 25,000 customers and approximately 41 million gallons of fuel.

During World War II, George Donovan again demonstrated his business flexibility by manufacturing hand grenades, building hemp mills and turning out 110-foot wooden submarine-chasers for the war effort. Over the years, Donovan's large construction projects have ranged from hospitals to colleges to high-rise office towers. Now the company has chosen to focus on electrical construction because the increasing demand for energy is an important factor.

While the Donovan Companies' annual report may suggest an all-business attitude among its owners, there is significant civic involvement, particularly in St. Paul church and educational institutions, by all four Donovan men. The efforts are quiet, however, and these vigorous Irishmen of St. Paul want to keep it that way.

A *Overhead maintenance*
B *Tower delivery*
C *Substation construction*
D *Underground installation*

Economics Laboratory, Inc.

Economics Laboratory, Inc., a multinational company with sales approaching $400 million, had its start in St. Paul in 1923, when Merritt J. Osborn, at the age of 44, invested $5,000 in a new idea.

M.J.'s first product was a carpet cleaner called ABSORBIT. With his second product, SOILAX, he pioneered the concept of product plus service for restaurant dishwashing. Today, the company specializes in developing and marketing products, systems and services for cleaning and environmental sanitation worldwide. Economics Laboratory, Inc., has operations in more than 52 countries of the world and it provides products for cleaning everything from jet engines to crystal glassware in the home.

Not once has family leadership of the company been broken since 1923. M.J. Osborn's son, E.B., joined the firm after graduating from Dartmouth College in 1928 and he is now chairman of the board. Fred T. Lanners, Jr., a 31-year company veteran with a background in chemical engineering and roots in St. Paul, is now president of Economics Laboratory, Inc.

Initially, manufacturing equipment for Economics Laboratory, Inc., was a mortar box, a five-pound scoop and a garden hoe. Today, not only is highly sophisticated manufacturing of products and equipment occurring in nine U.S. plants, it is also going on in 23 international locations.

Economics Laboratory, Inc., now manufactures products for a variety of institutions including hospitals, restaurants and hotels. The company also makes products for consumer use, especially for the home automatic dishwasher. Several key mergers in

A

the 1960's and 1970's broadened the company's marketing into food processing, dairy, transportation, marine, metalworking, the pulp and paper industries, laundry equipment and home coffee filters. Emphasis on research has always been an important part of Economics Laboratory, Inc., and in 1962 the Merritt J. Osborn Research and Development Center in Mendota Heights was dedicated. In 1968, the Osborn Building, a 20-story stainless steel and glass structure, became the company's worldwide headquarters. The project was the first building in St. Paul's downtown redevelopment district. Appropriately, the Osborn Building was designed with ultimate "cleanability" in mind, and observers often say that today's corporate home base of Economics Laboratory, Inc., lives up to the firm's major objective best — that is, a cleaner world.

A   *(Left to right) M.J. Osborn, founder, and his son, E.B. Osborn, who is now Chairman of the Board*

203

Farmers Union Central Exchange

A

The family farmer was a pressured businessman 40-50 years ago. He was often forced to pay premium prices for farm production supplies like fuel for his tractor and even for twine to bind his grain. One way to survive the high cost of doing business in those days was for farmers to organize cooperatively and to buy supplies together with neighbors.

Many farmers patronized small, locally-controlled retail cooperatives. But those co-ops were limited in their capabilities.

So, in the Depression year of 1931, CENEX was organized as a modest wholesale jobber of farm supplies by about 50 local retail cooperatives in the Midwest.

By forming CENEX, the farmer owners of these local co-ops were looking to lower the costs of their farm production supplies and to control their quality and availability through a wholesale cooperative that could purchase for them in large quantities.

CENEX opened for business in cramped, rented quarters in a downtown St. Paul office building with just $525 in cash, $26,000 in debts, and a $30,000 line of credit.

In 1935, headquarters were moved to a new site in South St. Paul near the Union Stockyards. From this location, farmers hauling their livestock to market could conveniently bring home CENEX supplies on their return trip.

Local cooperative retail service stations, grain elevators, feed mills, dairies and farmstores served by CENEX, began to operate in small towns all over the Midwest. Thanks to these co-ops, farmers were no longer forced to drive 50-100 miles to buy their supplies.

As the years passed, CENEX'S growing membership realized that even more money could be saved if the cooperative produced its own supplies such as gasoline, fuel oil, fertilizer, feed, seed, and manufactured items like hardware, machinery, and appliances.

Since the Second World War, CENEX has joined with other regional cooperatives in finding new sources of oil and in producing fertilizer for nearly every growing condition.

Today the cooperative that started with but $525 in 1931 has a net worth of approximately a quarter of a billion dollars and serves 1300 affiliated local cooperatives in 13 states with a complete line of farm supplies.

Although CENEX ranks among the 500 largest industrial corporations in the U.S., it is strictly a farmer-owned enterprise. Its bosses are 450,000 farm families who produce everything from milk to meat and wheat to wool. Their farms and ranches stretch from the shores of Lake Michigan to the Pacific Ocean.

CENEX'S 11-member board of directors is democratically elected by co-op members throughout the CENEX marketing area. These directors are all working farmers, many of whom are still serving on the boards of their own local cooperatives.

In five decades, CENEX has grown to become one of America's leading farm supply cooperatives. Throughout, CENEX has been a working partner with the people of St. Paul in sharing in the city's continued growth and development.

A   *One of the first oil wells owned by CENEX*

First National Bank of Saint Paul

A   B

C

Since its origin, the history of the First National Bank has been intertwined with the history of St. Paul. Considering the number of mergers that shaped today's First National Bank of Saint Paul, the chronology also provides a composite of city banking history. Over the years, more than 165 directors have guided affairs of the First Bank — among them, prominent business people and civic leaders like railroad "empire builder" James J. Hill, lumberman Frederick Weyerhaeuser and statesman Frank B. Kellogg. Philip H. Nason, retired Chairman of the Board, was a major force in the development of St. Paul's thriving Riverview Industrial Park and the revitalization of St. Paul's downtown area. In 1971, First National also demonstrated its faith in the future of downtown St. Paul by expanding and refurbishing its own headquarters.

Today, the First National Bank of Saint Paul is an influential factor in the economy of the Upper Midwest. Assets are in excess of $1.7 billion. Under the presidency of Clarence G. Frame, it continues its leadership role, not only in the business community but in significant community development and betterment projects, as well. Frame is also a director of First Bank System, Inc., of which First National is a member. This Twin City-based bank holding company includes 89 banks and trust companies and 113 offices in Minnesota, Wisconsin, the Dakotas and Montana. As the First National looks forward to the observance of its 125th birthday in 1978, one can well ponder over the great faith that Parker Paine had in the banking business and in the future of St. Paul.

In the 1850's, opening a bank was relatively easy. A man could literally become a banker just by hanging out a shingle and calling himself one. The business was primitive, at best. And in the pioneer community of St. Paul, money was scarce and settlers had little faith in banks of any kind. Parker Paine, the handsome, fur-trading entrepreneur from Vermont, however, had great faith in the banking business. And he had plans for the burgeoning little community called St. Paul. Paine knew all about the vast Sioux Indian lands that had opened up in Minnesota for settlement. He was also encouraged when he arrived by steamboat in 1853 and saw a crowd of newcomers ready to make their new lives in St. Paul.

With less than $40,000 in capital, Paine started his bank. Along with conventional currency, beaver pelts were probably a popular medium of exchange, too. (Sometimes those pelts were considered more stable than cash). Six years later, two Southerners, James and Horace Thompson, joined Paine and proved to be able bankers, too. By 1863, they assumed control of Paine's enterprise and applied for a national charter. With that, the First National Bank of Saint Paul was created with capital of $250,000 in the first year.

A   *First National's downtown facility*
B   *The 1886 banking lobby*
C   *Founder Paine's first office*

Foley Brothers, Inc.

A

B

The four young men who founded Foley Brothers, Inc., of St. Paul were resolute businessmen who learned their toughness in the Canadian wilds more than 100 years ago. There Timothy, Thomas, John and Michael Foley learned lumbering the hard way from their father, John. At age ten, Tim Foley took a team to the woods for winter logging, and, in their teens, all four Foley boys rode log drives down turbulent waterways to waiting lumber mills.

It was the four boys who founded the business in 1875, and brought the Foley business to St. Paul in 1887. Not long afterward, the enterprising quartet discovered that the same horse-drawn teams used for logging could also handle grading and earth-moving during the summer. With that new application, Foley Brothers moved into the construction business — its specialty today. The timing of this new diversity was ideal. By the late 1800's, railroad construction was well under way. Isolated lines became branches and branches became complex networks carrying people and cargo all over the United States and Canada. Foley Brothers was part of it all and, in total, the firm built about 25,000 miles of railway at a total cost of more than one billion dollars. All along, the Foley brothers were operating out of stalwart stone structures in downtown St. Paul called the Gilfillan Block, the New York Building, and the Endicott Building.

With the close of World War I, however, the era of railroad building also ended. The founding Foleys, advanced in age, died in those waning years and company leadership was left to Edward T. Foley, Michael Foley's son, and Frank J. Anderson, Michael's son-in-law. During that period, Foley Brothers completed one of St. Paul's grandest

landmarks — the Saint Paul Cathedral. That work led to other local projects, including construction of the St. Paul Union Depot, a new administration building for St. Thomas College, Nazareth Hall, Ramsey County Courthouse and City Hall, the New Brighton Arsenal, the Minneapolis-St. Paul International Airport Terminal, the Erie Mining Taconite Plant, and the Prairie Island Nuclear Generating Plant. Today, Foley Brothers has moved into a new realm of construction. Horses and mules have been replaced by the diesel engine; and transcontinental railroad building has been supplanted by construction of complex industrial plants, huge dams and highways. And although a majority of its work is now outside the Twin Cities area, Foley Brothers maintains its strong connection to St. Paul. The successors to the founders of the Company and to the management of the 20's through 50's are now William H. Lang, George C. Lindquist, David E. Anderson, John F. Youngstrom, and Halbert L. Wall.

C

D

E

A *Horse-drawn log sled.*
B *Early office at Foley, Minn.*
C *Shasta Dam.*
D *Prairie Island Nuclear Generating Plant.*
E *Square Butte Electric Plant.*

H.B. Fuller Company

A

B

Harvey Benjamin Fuller had a grand design. Perhaps it didn't seem so grand when he cooked his first batch of wallpaper paste on a kitchen stove in St. Paul more than 90 years ago. But it was. Harvey sold his paste to local paperhangers and a handful of bookbinders. His customers arrived in horse-drawn wagons at Fuller's first office on Robert Street and waited patiently as their paste was transferred from the third floor ''manufacturing plant'' to the ground via a hand-operated elevator. Those early clients counted on Harvey, especially during the spring decorating season.

But Harvey Fuller was inventive by nature and he didn't stop at paste. Harvey and his two sons, Albert and H.B., Jr., explored other products — paints, for example, and steel scaffolding for painters, paperhangers and other tradesmen. It was this enthusiasm for innovation that survived long after the senior Fuller died.

Today, Harvey Benjamin Fuller's firm has diversified widely and annual sales, worldwide, now approach $200 million. Although adhesives, sealants and coatings are still the major products manufactured by this long-time St. Paul firm, other product lines have been added, including paints, floor maintenance equipment, sanitation chemicals and specialty waxes for various markets. The paste that once seemed to be no more than a modest mixture of flour and water has been adapted and refined into a variety of specialized adhesives. And the modest paste wagon carrying 2,000-pound barrels and pulled by ''Davey,'' the workhorse, has been replaced by rail, freight cars and truck fleets.

During the firm's lengthy history, the man most responsible for H.B. Fuller's growth is Elmer L. Andersen, current Chairman of the Board and Governor of Minnesota from 1961 to 1963. Andersen was hired to be H.B. Fuller's advertising director in the early 1930's and later bought the business from the Fuller family in hopes of keeping the essential management intact, despite offers by other interests to buy the company. Andersen's leadership is characterized by a personalized concern for employees and a heightened emphasis on corporate social responsibility. H.B. Fuller employees are encouraged to pursue their interest and involvement in the community, and the corporation contributes five percent of its U.S. pre-tax earnings to civic causes. With H.B. Fuller's commitment to double sales and earnings every five years, the philanthropic sum is substantial . . . and growing.

A *Founder H.B. Fuller*
B *Early delivery trucks*

Grain Terminal Association

A

B

St. Paul was a friend of agriculture from the very beginning. In the early 1900's, the city fathers knew that farmers needed their own grain marketing system. Farmers had successfully organized local co-op grain elevators, but they ran into real obstacles when they tried to organize on a regional basis for their own benefit. During that era, stories about abuses aimed at farmers by marketing middlemen were legend. In 1906, alone, farmers reportedly lost as much as $5 million annually because of inequities in the marketing of their grain. So the city of St. Paul established a grain exchange for farmers in the early 1900's and, although the enterprise was short-

lived due to poor market conditions, the climate for cooperative thinking in St. Paul was supportive, indeed.

After those first years of discouragement, amplified by the Depression, the Grain Terminal Association (GTA) was finally formed in St. Paul on a hopeful afternoon in 1938. The organization was bolstered by 121 local grain cooperatives whose members cast their lot with GTA . . . and with a $30,000 loan offered by another friendly St. Paul supply co-op. Thanks to Farm Security (FHA) loans in the following year, GTA farmers were able to finance another 120 local elevators in Minnesota, the Dakotas and Wisconsin. GTA was off and running.

In its first full year of operation, the regional grain co-op handled 17 million bushels of wheat, rye and barley and saved member farmers $144,000. The savings were substantial because in those early years, farmers could not expect the crop yield they do today. Managing the efforts of GTA from year one was M.W. Thatcher. This man — who has been credited with many of the advances achieved by the cooperative — did not retire from his post as GTA general manager until 1968 at age 85.

Today, 150,000 farm families are GTA members and more than 600 grain elevators are part of the co-op network. In 1976, alone, GTA handled approximately 282 million bushels of grain, sold 249,000 tons of feed and saved more than $15 million for members. GTA President B.J. Malusky and Chairman of the Board Jewell Haaland reported in 1976 that GTA saved member farmers almost $189 million during the co-op's 38-year history. Not only is GTA in the marketing of grain today, but it has also joined with other regional cooperatives in a barge transport business and an export company for international marketing. In addition, GTA has joined with other Twin Cities co-ops to form a large vehicle and farm equipment pool. Today, GTA ranks among the largest grain marketing and processing co-ops in the world. That, says President B.J. Malusky, represents quite an advance since 1938 when a handful of grain farmers cast their lot together.

A *Grain Terminal Association entrance*
B *Massive river terminal during the 1940's*

Hoerner Waldorf

A

B

C

Since its beginning in 1886, Hoerner Waldorf, a division of Champion International Corporation, has been a leader in the packaging industry. Long before consumer products were as sophisticated as they are today, H.L. Collins was producing labels and pill boxes at his modest Fifth and Minnesota Street plant in downtown St. Paul. Whether he realized it or not, Collins was in on the ground floor of what was to become a diverse and expansive paper products industry in which Hoerner Waldorf would become a major producer. Collins' labels led to corrugated shipping containers. Cartons led to consumer packages and shopping bags designed to provide for the protection and convenient handling of everything from an ounce of fishfood to a week's load of groceries.

Today, Hoerner Waldorf ranks among the top six producers in the U.S. paper packaging industry. During its history, the original company founded by Collins has been involved in several mergers and expansion plans. In 1977, however, the most notable merger occurred when Hoerner Waldorf joined Champion International Corp. of Stamford, Connecticut, one of the two largest forest products companies in the world. Hoerner Waldorf is now the packaging business unit of Champion with its headquarters remaining in the Midway district of St. Paul. Today, the massive paper mills in St. Paul produce 710 tons of paper products daily compared to approximately 40 tons per day in early years. And paper board produced in three other Hoerner Waldorf mills in Montana, Michigan, and North Carolina bring the total daily output to approximately 3,330 tons.

Most of Hoerner Waldorf's 2,275 Minnesota employees work at the St. Paul complex and the company's payroll in this state comes to almost $35 million per year.

Early in Hoerner Waldorf's history, recovery of paper products and waste wood became an important priority and it remains a priority today in this age of environmental awareness. Adults whose childhoods date to the early 1920's in St. Paul remember the massive paper drives involving thousands of children inaugurated by Hoerner Waldorf. Today, Hoerner Waldorf is considered one of the nation's largest recyclers, annually converting about 215,000 tons of wastepaper into packaging material.

A   *Hoerner Waldorf pioneered massive paper drives at Margaret Fuller School, 1923*
B   *Douglas School, Minneapolis, 1922*
C   *Scheffer School, 1923*

Hoffmann Electric

A

Most St. Paul homes in 1910 were lighted with piped-in gas ... and residents could thank Robert Wilhelm Bunsen and Carl von Welsbach for that. Bunsen developed what is widely known in high school science labs across the country as the Bunsen Burner and Welsbach invented a cover for that open flame, making it suitable for home lighting.

About the time Welsbach was perfecting his innovative '' Welsbach mantle,'' R.D.Hoffmann, a St. Paul man who was to make lighting a life-time business, was born. In fact, as a young man, Hoffmann became one of the first salesmen for the developing Welsbach Company. In time, however, Hoffmann became restless. It was okay to sell mantles for someone else, he thought. It was even gratifying to be singled-out as the next sales manager for Welsbach in Chicago. But why leave St. Paul? Why not start a business of your own and stay, he reasoned.

Hoffmann did precisely that in 1910. He located a few skilled electricians and set to work selling the young company's services. At first, gas was the dominant source of light, but electricity was coming on strong. People soon recognized the safety and convenience of electric light and Ray Hoffmann capitalized on it.

Since Ray Hoffmann founded the business on West Seventh Street in St. Paul, his sons Edward and Richard have managed the firm during its evolution over approximately 68 years. Each of the three Hoffmanns have logged about 27 years in the lighting business. Today, Hoffmann Electric is the oldest electrical contracting company in St. Paul and one of the largest in the Midwest. Most of the firm's business is now concentrated on commercial and industrial accounts and notable recent projects in St. Paul have included lighting Interstate Highways 94 and 35E, wiring portions of the 3M complex, the new Ramsey-Gillette Hospital, the West Seventh Street senior citizens high rise, the McKnight Geriatric Home in Arden Hills, and William Mitchell Law School on Summit Avenue. Most recently, Hoffmann was selected to handle Central High School, the St. Paul Radisson Hotel, and a four million dollar project at the Metropolitan Waste Water Treatment Center in St. Paul. Hoffmann Electric also has a wholly-owned subsidiary called Nu-Comp Systems, Inc., a data processing service handling the record keeping for a number of small banks in the Twin Cities.

Since 1890, the Hoffmann family has lived in St. Paul and, says President Dick Hoffmann, they have no intention of leaving.

Other officers are Vice President Don Dolan, Secretary Tom Kolias, and Treasurer Mars Hagen.

A *Representative Hoffmann commercial and industrial clients.*

Kraus-Anderson of St. Paul Co.

Kraus-Anderson of St. Paul Co. was established in 1949, to maintain a close and personalized relationship with the expanding St. Paul business community. Since that time, the St. Paul firm has operated out of the same office at Grand and Seventh for nearly 30 years, and it has constructed a number of notable city landmarks. Dayton's Department Store is probably the most visible downtown anchor built by Kraus-Anderson of St. Paul Co. In addition, the company has immersed itself in the city's history by accepting significant restoration projects of historic St. Paul buildings. Mattock School, for example, was a quaint red stone landmark remembered by many St. Paul residents who spent their early years there. In 1962, St. Paul school officials asked Kraus-Anderson to supervise Mattock's restoration and preservation. The company painstakingly dismantled the 93-year-old school — stone by stone — at its original site near the intersection of Randolph and Snelling and reconstructed it adjacent to the Highland junior and senior high schools in Highland Park.

Recently, Kraus-Anderson restored the 105-year-old Victorian mansion on Exchange Street, once owned by St. Paul dry-goods merchant and shoe manufacturer, Joseph Lybrandt Forepaugh. The multi-story building is situated across the street from the Ramsey House, the home of Minnesota's first governor, Alexander Ramsey. After his death, Forepaugh's mansion became a rooming house, then stood vacant for years before Bill Naegele of Restaurants No Limit decided to buy it and turn it into a three-story restaurant. During the long restoration job, Kraus-Anderson of St. Paul Co. found debris left from years of disuse, but behind it they also found ornate and rare evidence of an era long gone.

The St. Paul Office is part of the Twin City-based Kraus-Anderson operations which provide construction, construction management, development, and real estate leasing services throughout the United States. The combined company is among the 400 largest construction firms in the United States.

A/H   *Kraus-Anderson of St. Paul Co. is helping make history live. Recent significant restoration projects include Mattock School and the 105-year-old former mansion home of Joseph Lybrandt Forepaugh*

A

B

C

D

E

F

G

H

KSTP Radio/TV

A

B

C

Never before had a radio station been so honored. It was March 29, 1928. Accompanied by a trumpet fanfare and a Sousa march, President Calvin Coolidge pressed a tiny button in his White House office 1,062 miles away and officially put KSTP Radio on the air. Staff members at the studios inside the Hotel St. Paul were thrilled. So were their counterparts in a neighborhood studio across the river in the Radisson Hotel, Minneapolis. But happiest of all was Stanley E. Hubbard, pioneer broadcaster, salesman and commercial flyer, who created KSTP and is still, today, the station's Chairman of the Board. (The company has since grown from one station to eight high-powered radio and television stations.)

Hubbard was a product of the University of Minnesota and started his business career selling cars afternoons and Saturdays while attending Central High School in St. Paul. After the war he started the Mattingly-Hubbard Motor Company in Louisville, Kentucky, which also had an airplane division.

In 1919 Mr. Hubbard created the Ohio Valley Aero Transport Company with air service from Louisville to Cincinnati. This was the first commercial airline in the United States. In 1923 Mr. Hubbard entered the radio business with Station WAMD in Minneapolis, which was the first commercial radio station in the United States. In that era there were other radio stations, but they existed as promotional vehicles for their company owners. In 1928 a fire at the transmitter destroyed the station's facilities; but with financial backing from the National

Battery Company, Hubbard managed to start the current KSTP.

The inauguration of Hubbard's new station in 1928 was unparalleled . . . and Minnesota leaders knew it. Appearing on the first live broadcast were Minnesota Lieutenant Governor W.I. Nolan; the Mayor of St. Paul, L.C. (Larry Ho) Hodgson; Lytton J. Shields, president of the National Battery Broadcasting Company; and St. Paul Business spokesman, William Davidson. The announcer was Kenneth Hance. The all-music program was replete with optimistic tunes including "The Land of Hope and Glory" and "There Must Be a Silver Lining."

In those early years, KSTP was a source of news, information and entertainment Twin Citians had never heard before. Amos and Andy were introduced and even those at movie houses insisted on a broadcast break to hear their favorite comedy pair. KSTP brought the first network programs to the Twin Cities. Mr. Hubbard was the Regional Chairman of the Atwater Kent auditions which created talent for both the Metropolitan Opera and radio. Many of the winners of the auditions became top personalitites not only in the Metropolitan Opera but also on national broadcasting.

KSTP was the first station in the United States to establish a full-time news department and a radio news wire. The station demonstrated its sense of humor while covering the St. Paul Open Golf Tournament with a radio transmitter tucked in a baby carriage. Broadcasters from KSTP earned national attention when they covered the 1937 floods that ripped through Cairo, Illinois. By 1938,

212

D

E

F

G

Stanley Hubbard had purchased a television camera produced by RCA and carried on closed circuit experiments for many years. At one time, KSTP broadcast a special Legion parade in Minneapolis which was the first parade ever televised.

By 1948, KSTP went on the air with regularly scheduled TV broadcasts and it became the first TV station operating between Chicago and the West Coast. Hubbard illustrated his faith in the growing operation by building a new facility on University Avenue and a 601-foot tower to broadcast KSTP's 110,000-watt signal where St. Paul and Minneapolis meet. (Hubbard diplomatically picked the site to maintain his friendship with both cities. Not surprisingly, the Twin Cities boundary line actually runs through the middle of the KSTP building.)

Under Hubbard's leadership, the station has garnered a number of other broadcasting firsts — first NBC TV affiliate, established in 1948; first 10 p.m. news program on a seven-day schedule, inaugurated in 1950; first color television program broadcast, in 1954; and the first independent station in the United States with full color programming, in 1960.

Over the years, KSTP carried St. Paul events to its listeners and viewers in unmatched ways — notable among them were St. Paul Winter Carnival parades broadcast for at least four decades. That station also performed a special kind of outreach for the city when it carried St. Paul broadcaster David Stone and his Sunset Valley Barn Dance to little towns all over Minnesota, Wisconsin, and the Dakotas. The effect of on-location hoe downs was memorably colorful. That's entertainment.

Today, as in the 20's when radio was first beginning, KSTP television and radio continue leadership with the first "ActionCam" coverage in the upper Midwest on its news programs, and the first weather services department with Weather Surveillance Radar, Laserfax Weather Satellite Picture Receiver, and a Weather Observer Network. In their efforts to offer quality programming of timely importance to Twin Cities area viewers, KSTP has introduced new programs such as SKYWATCH, a 24-hour weather reporting service used during periods of threatening weather, and agricultural programs to fulfill the current needs of the viewing community.

A *KSTP on-the-scene TV telecasts.*
B *Back Row: Bert Lahr, James Cagney, Frances Langford, and Stanley E. Hubbard (Chairman of the Board, KSTP).*
   Front Row: Merle Oberon, Frank McHugh, and Pat O'Brien.
C *President Coolidge officially puts KSTP Radio on the air.*
D *First business of KSTP's founder, Stanley Hubbard.*
E *KSTP's "Newshawk."*
F *Live broadcast of golf tournament.*
G *ActionCam unit in field ready for live coverage.*

The Lindsay Division of Ecodyne Corporation

For decades, residents of the Upper Midwest learned to live with hard water, iron-rich water, and acid water. It stained their plumbing fixtures, frequently discolored their laundry, and sometimes altered the taste of their food. At first, not much could be done about it. Water was water, and early water-treatment equipment was expensive, complex, bulky, and designed mainly for commercial and industrial uses.

Knowing that Twin Cities residents and businesses needed quality water, Lyn G. Lindsay began in the 1920's to improve cumbersome water-conditioning equipment. Laundries, hotels, and institutions had just begun using "Zeolite" water softeners utilizing processed "green sand" as a conditioning mineral. By 1925, simple water softeners operating on the same principal were installed in a few homes as well. Improvements emerged fast; however, an inventive Lyn Lindsay

Water softener sales were limited in the Twenties and Thirties. The Depression put a number of firms out of business and Lindsay wisely put his enterprise temporarily aside.

Mr. Lindsay returned to his soft-water business in 1940, joined by his two sons Jim and Lyn, Jr., and five years later founded what is known today as The Lindsay Division in suburban St. Paul.

Fortunately, Mr. Lindsay remained determined during these tough years. Even though water-softening equipment in some form had been available for nearly 20 years, only 2,000 homeowners in the country purchased units in 1941. With postwar development of smaller and more efficient models, however, sales skyrocketed. In 1950, an estimated 167,000 water softeners were sold and one year later the Lindsay Company recorded its first million-dollar business year.

The company introduced, on a large scale, the first automatic domestic water-conditioner in 1953. This innovation, which seems so natural today, marked a new era in the growth of the home water-conditioning market.

A

B

C

developed a number of major improvements of his own.

Water supplied by municipalities, while potable, requires additional treatment to remove dissolved minerals that prevent the proper cleaning action of soap, cause mineral deposits in plumbing and fixtures, and contribute to excessive water usage. Water entering a home is often conditioned to remove these minerals prior to use. A water conditioner removes hardness minerals and results in water that cleans better, tastes better, and looks clearer.

Lindsay pioneered a number of industry innovations during the 1950's and 60's. They introduced a high capacity resin for softeners in 1950, fiberglass pressure tanks in 1955, first console (tank within a tank) unit in 1958, and the first iron-free softening system in 1963. In 1977, the company introduced the first convertible water-conditioning unit in the industry.

Today, the Lindsay Company is the largest manufacturer of automatic water conditioning equipment in the United States and is growing at a rate of about 22% annually. About 85% of the homes in the U.S. have some water problems of hardness, iron, acidity, bad taste, or odor.

The current President of Lindsay is Gerald T. Shannon who became chief executive officer of the firm in 1972. In his short tenure he has made an indelible mark on Lindsay and the industry at large. Recently, Mr. Shannon was given additional responsibility when he was appointed Vice President of Ecodyne Corporation, Lindsay's parent company.

Shannon, a former pilot with the U.S. Navy during World War II, is currently a member of the Board of Directors of the St. Paul Chamber of Commerce, a Director of the St. Paul Employers Association and a member of Rotary International.

In the water-conditioning industry, Mr. Shannon has been on the Board of Governors of the Water Quality Association since he came into the industry and is now Vice President of the group. He has been influential in guiding the current and long range positions for the water-conditioning industry. Under Shannon's leadership, Lindsay has become one of the most progressive and profitable manufacturing companies in the water conditioning industry.

The Lindsay Company is now a Division of Ecodyne Corporation, an affiliate of Trans Union Corporation. When Ecodyne was formed by Trans Union, it became one of the largest groups of companies specializing in equipment designed for handling and treating water and wastewater.

Lindsay's large and modern chemistry laboratory recently installed an automated water-analysis system utilizing a computer controlled atomic absorption spectrophotometer. The system is capable of testing 200 water samples every six seconds and distinguishing 50 different elements in each sample. The company performed over 300,000 individual water tests during the last year.

Although water softeners still comprise a major part of Lindsay's business, the firm has diversified widely. Lindsay furnishes equipment for residential and commercial applications which purifies and renews poor-quality water by removing undesirable hardness, iron, color, taste, odor, and sediment. The company custom-designs water softening equipment for a number of clients; the firm also develops and sells iron removers, taste and odor filters, package demineralizers, and reverse osmosis and deionization equipment used to prepare water for "high-quality-demand" settings such as hospitals.

Lindsay has continued to develop new products, one of which is a line of chemicals designed as sequestering agents to prevent such reactions as scale formation, corrosion, and discoloration. Primary application is in the treatment of home water supplies, laundries, boilers, water cooling towers, food-processing plants, and municipalities.

The Lindsay Division also operates Mec-O-Matic, a producer of chemical feed pumps for swimming-pool water treatment, for the chlorination of home well-water supplies, and for large automatic dishwashing and automobile washing equipment. In 1976 alone, the value of water conditioning equipment and chemical feed pumps sold by Lindsay to residential and commercial users totaled more than $24 million.

A   *Lyn G. Lindsay, Sr.*
B   *Gerald T. Shannon*
C   *Present "heavy-duty" water conditioner*
D   *Current plant in Woodlane*
E   *First Lindsay building, downtown St. Paul, circa 1945*

D

E

W. A. Lang Co.

Working out of an obscure basement office in St. Paul, W.A. Lang began selling fire and tornado insurance to the homeowners and business people of his town in 1909. There was no such thing as general liability insurance, but memories of the San Francisco earthquake and fire just three years before made insurance seem more essential. Lang depended on that. He developed a fine class of business, including some of the most influential companies in St. Paul and many railroad owners who recognized that St. Paul was a major center for passenger and freight activity. In those days, any business worth more than $100,000 was very big, indeed . . . and W.A. Lang was there with appropriate insurance protection.

Lang knew his enterprise well. Right after graduation from the University of Minnesota in 1881, Lang went to work for St. Paul Fire and Marine Insurance Company. For more than 20 years, he worked at the "City Desk", selling insurance directly to the public. When the firm stopped selling its own policies, it gave W. A. Lang the exclusive right to sell St. Paul Fire and Marine policies in St. Paul. Lang set up shop in the company's basement and later acted as an agent for ten other major insurance companies as well.

During the early years, Lang worked with a very small staff, including George W. Elliott, Lang's "custodian of cash" who earned a whopping $115 a month in the early 1900's. Elliott continued to work with Lang for 40 years.

Thanks to a growing need for insurance by St. Paul residents and businesses, Lang's enterprise grew. New kinds of specialized insurance emerged, and, in the eleven years from 1909 to 1920, total premiums paid to the Lang company doubled from $216,000 to $464,000. By 1948, Lang topped the $1 million mark. Mr. Lang remained active in the business until his death in 1950.

Today, W.A. Lang Co. has its own office in the Hanover Building in downtown St. Paul and still represents four of the original insurance companies that W. A. handled in the early years. The current firm specializes in all types of insurance provided by many of the major American companies. W.A. Lang now has approximately 12,000 policyholders and annual premiums in excess of $10 million. The firm

A

does business all over the United States and in some foreign countries. W.A. Lang's son, William H., former Vice President of the firm, is still a member of the company's Board of Directors, and Ernest Collingham, who was an office boy when he started with Lang in 1931, is now President and Chairman of the Board. As it has for almost 70 years, W. A. Lang continues to represent quality insurance protection.

A   *Founder William A. Lang*

McGill/Printing, Inc.

A

B   C

A   *McGill's front office at Cedar and 8th, 1898.*
B   *Governor Andrew R. McGill.*
C   *Frank Beddor, Jr., Chairman of the Board*

As the oldest printing firm in the area, McGill/Printing, Inc., has shared in the dynamic growth of St. Paul and the surrounding area.

It all began for McGill in 1848 when the Pioneer printing plant was established at Third and Minnesota streets in downtown St. Paul. A year later, its noteworthy owner, newspaper editor J. N. Goodhue, published the first copy of the Pioneer Newspaper. As was common in those days, printing plants published newspapers and did commercial printing, too. In 1875, the company name was changed to the Pioneer Press.

Twenty-four years later, Eli S. Warner and Charles H. McGill of the McGill-Warner Company became associated with the company, buying part interest in the Pioneer Press Printing Co. And, in 1909, the two men acquired all remaining interests of the company. The McGill-Warner plant was located at 9th and Sibley streets at that time.

The McGill family had a lengthy history of Minnesota involvement. Andrew R. McGill, father of C.H. McGill, was Governor of the State of Minnesota from 1887 to 1889 and was also affiliated with McGill-Warner Company.

As time passed, the expanded McGill-Warner Company proved to be printing industry leaders by bringing Monotype to Minnesota — a major advance. The introduction of this method for producing machine-set type was a boon to the business and quickly replaced the tedious hand-setting method. In addition, McGill-Warner was first in the state to operate a lithograph press.

Over its 129 years, the company has been owned by several families. In 1963, Norman B. Mears of the Buckbee Mears Company acquired the company and most recently, in 1976, the company was taken over by Frank Beddor, Jr., then owner of Printing, Inc., in Minneapolis. Today the company is called McGill/Printing, Inc., and it is located in the Midway area of St. Paul on Fairview Avenue.

Under its new, young and aggressive management, McGill/Printing, Inc., has shown rapid growth. One of the goals for the future is a new capital improvement plan, replacing present machinery with the very latest in high speed printing equipment. The company specializes in quality four-color advertising literature, catalogs and newspaper inserts.

Minnesota Federal Savings and Loan Association

A

B

It was a hot summer day in 1922 when a group of Twin Cities businessmen gathered in a small office in downtown St. Paul. Their goal: to form a new local financial organization dedicated to helping hard-working, thrifty members of the community save money and build or purchase homes.

From that small beginning grew Minnesota Federal, which has gone on to become one of the largest and most progressive savings and loan associations in the entire nation, and the only major Minnesota firm of its type headquartered in St. Paul.

Shortly after that initial meeting, the first mortgage loan was approved . . . for $4,500 on a home in Litchfield. By the end of that first year's business, resources totalled only $11,200 — not an electrifying start, but the idea had caught on. The concept of a local thrift institution, based on sound, time-tested financial principles and offering a safe

haven for funds with a high rate of return, appealed to the people of the Twin Cities and surrounding area, and the association grew rapidly.

Since that early start, Minnesota Federal has increased its rate of growth impressively across the years. The $100-million mark in assets was reached in 1955. In 1967 assets reached the $300-million mark, and in 1977 they stood at $850 million. The firm serves its 220,000 savings customers and 28,000 home loan customers through twenty-nine locations in the metropolitan area plus outstate offices at Red Wing, Rochester and St. Cloud. Those three outstate offices, incidentally, were the first authorized by the Federal Home Loan Bank board for a major Twin Cities savings and loan association.

To keep pace with this rapid growth, several changes in home office location were necessary over the years, but offices in the St. Paul loop were always within the general area of Fifth and Minnesota, where the two-story, 27,000-square-foot Minnesota Federal building now stands. Nearby, at Fourth and Minnesota, is the well-known Minnesota Federal Plaza, where thousands of spectators have enjoyed free outdoor entertainment programs sponsored as a community service by the firm.

Two other Minnesota Federal offices also are located within the city. The Macalester-Groveland office, at Grand and Macalester avenues, serves the Midway district, and the Phalen Park office, near Phalen Shopping Center, serves the city's east side. In the city's immediate suburban ring are Minnesota Federal's Mendota Heights, Roseville, Shoreview, White Bear Lake and Woodbury offices.

Minnesota Federal has deep roots within our state — roots which became even deeper in 1975 when the firm merged with Red Wing Federal, whose beginnings date back to April, 1877. Yet management has its outlook firmly geared to the future, constantly seeking out new ways to improve and broaden service to Minnesota Federal's customers. Such progress, however, will always be based on the same principles of thrift and home ownership that across the years have become Minnesota Federal's trademark in doing business with the public.

A *Winter Marching Unit, 1940.*
B *New neighborhood office.*

The Minnesota Mutual Life Insurance Company

A

B

C

Russell R. Dorr knew St. Paul in the 1880's was a prime place to start a business. The city was humming with commercial, financial and railway activity. Thousands of land-hungry immigrants and enterprising Easterners were heading to the Midwest in search of new opportunities. They would need insurance.

One hot morning in August of 1880, Dorr met with eight St. Paul businessmen in Room 15 of a building at Jackson and Third. It was the office of Charles Bigelow, president of St. Paul Fire and Marine Insurance Company, Minnesota's oldest corporation.

Together Dorr and his colleagues laid plans for an assessment insurance firm that later became The Minnesota Mutual Life Insurance Company, the largest Minnesota-based insurance company that also ranks 16th among all U.S. life insurance companies. Today, Minnesota Mutual Life has assets exceeding $1 billion and serves more than

four million people whose policies total $25 billion of life insurance in force.

In the early years, insured members were expected to pay their fair share when a member died — that was the essence of the assessment process. In time, however, that method proved unrealistic for most insurance companies and Minnesota Mutual Life converted to a level premium, legal reserve company. Several years later, Eugene Randall, former farmhand, country schoolteacher, high school principal and newspaper editor, became president of Minnesota Mutual Life. Over the years, he became fondly known as the "Grand Old Man of Minnesota Mutual." One of his successors, Harold J. Cummings, guided the firm for nearly 30 years and watched the enterprise move toward becoming one of the largest financial institutions in the region. When Minnesota Mutual Life reached $1 billion of insurance in force by 1953, Cummings and his employees joined together to buy a single premium educational endowment policy for a six-month-old Chicago orphan. In future years, three more children became special Minnesota Mutual Life beneficiaries as billion-dollar benchmarks were attained.

Minnesota Mutual Life has always been a St. Paul resident and completion of its current headquarters in St. Paul in 1955 was particularly important. After nearly 25 years of minimal construction in downtown St. Paul, groundbreaking for Minnesota Mutual Life represented a new vote of confidence in the downtown area and symbolized a rebirth for development in downtown St. Paul.

Currently, Minnesota Mutual Life is headed by Coleman Bloomfield, president and chief executive officer.

A   *Minnesota Mutual's original offices*
B & C   *Early life insurance assessment policy*

The Murphy Companies

In the early 1900s, freight piling up in the railroad yards and the river landing at the foot of Jackson Street caught the attention of an enterprising Irishman, E.L. Murphy, prominent in city affairs as an alderman from the Rice Street area. What was needed by the wholesale companies crowding the old business district, Murphy decided, was some help in moving freight from the levee and the railroad yards to the jobbers.

Matching demand with supply, Murphy and his son, a second E.L. Murphy, launched their own transportation business, Murphy Transfer and Storage, in 1904 with one horse and one wagon. Today the grandsons of the first Murphy are now in command of what has grown into a cluster of transportation and warehousing companies, and their distinctive emerald-green trucks are familiar to everyone who drives the nation's highways.

C

A

B

By 1910 E.L. Murphy had introduced what are believed to be the first motorized trucks into St. Paul. By 1916, the firm had assembled its first trucking fleet, 23 red and yellow rigs that were fondly nicknamed "Murphy's circus wagons." The Murphys next became the first trucking company to expand operations into serving cities beyond St. Paul and Minneapolis. Their trucks hauled freight of all kinds throughout Minnesota and Wisconsin, and since snow-clogged roads were common, they equipped their trucks with plows to clear the routes. The word seeped through the community and during bad weather people gathered to follow the plow-equipped trucks out of town.

Murphy Motor Freight Lines was established in 1913 to expand intercity hauling. The business now operates over more than 8,533 regular route miles from the Dakotas to New York, and it serves 1,316 communities in 12 states on a daily basis.

Next came E.L. Murphy Trucking Company, which was founded in 1936 to handle the hauling of freight in the Twin Cities area but has since been expanded into a nation-wide heavy specialized carrier serving the lower 48 states.

Murphy Warehouse Company was established twenty years later, in 1956, to store goods of every description in its million-square feet of space.

Two more companies were set up in 1967; Murphy Rigging and Erecting Company, which moves, installs, and dismantles all types of iron, steel, and machinery, and Murphy Delivery Service, which handles local contract hauling work within the Murphy Companies' grouping. Annual revenues for all the companies now exceed $85 million.

The management of the five Murphy companies is still based in St. Paul and it is still in the family — in the hands of two third-generation Murphys. They are Edward L. Murphy, Jr., and Richard T. Murphy, the sons of E.L. Murphy, Sr., who, with his father, founded the entire enterprise.

Both Edward and Richard grew up in the business, working at truck driving and other odd jobs. Today, they both serve on the Executive Committee of the American Trucking Associations, and they are active in St. Paul civic enterprises. In keeping with their strong St. Paul Irish heritage, they are noted throughout the business community for their green-carpeted offices.

A *Today's Murphy Motor Freight Lines truck.*
B *Today's E.L. Murphy Trucking Co. truck.*
C *Early Murphy wagon and team.*

Mutual Service Insurance

For more than half a century, farmers have known that adversity leads to cooperation. They watched the Depression force prices to pitiful extremes — eggs sold for six cents a dozen and wheat brought 33 cents a bushel in 1932. They slipped deep into debt and saw many of their friends and neighbors forced out of farming altogether. They suffered drought and dust blizzards and adverse economic conditions.

One way to survive, they found, was to help each other by banding together into cooperatives. There were cooperative creameries and grain elevators and stockyards; and there were co-ops for buying feed, seed, fertilizer, petroleum products, and groceries. If a barn burned, it was probably covered under a cooperative arrangement called a township mutual fire insurance society.

As motor vehicles became part of farming operations, it was inevitable that cooperative auto insurance would become available. From that point it was easy to see cooperative life insurance in the picture.

Five of these small insurance companies eventually pooled their field forces and then in 1949 became a single organization, now known as Mutual Service Insurance, with headquarters in St. Paul. The first president was Felix F. Rondeau, who, as a young man from rural Wisconsin, led the original companies through the years of consolidation. With his retirement in 1970, leadership was passed to W.L. Sanford, who died five months later. He was succeeded by Roman N. Eller in December of 1970, current president and chief executive officer.

Insurance operations are handled through three companies; Mutual Service Life Insurance Company, Mutual Service Casualty Insurance Company, and Modern Service Insurance Company. The "people helping people" philosophy now extends well beyond the original rural market and the companies are represented by more than 500 local agents in a 23-state operating territory. Annual premium income now is more than $100 million and life insurance in force exceeds $1.4 billion, placing it in the top 14% of all life insurance companies in the United States. All three are rated A + by Best's — one of the country's leading insurance financial rating services.

A   *Mutual's three company presidents*
B   *The first St. Paul office*
C   *Mid-30's office-shared building*
D   *One of company's first offices*

A

C

B

D

The North Central Companies, Inc.

A

B

The advertisement made a good case for local investment in the 1920's: "Why buy your insurance from a firm outside Minnesota?" the ad asked. "Why send $33 million annually to 'foreign' life insurance companies?"

That line of reasoning made good sense to many Minnesotans who heeded the advertisement and began buying "home-grown" life insurance from the Modern Life Company, predecessor of what is known today as The North Central Companies, Inc.

The founders of Modern Life had special respectability because the company's first president was J.A.A. Burnquist, former Minnesota Governor and Attorney General. Another of Modern Life's first Board members and second president also had special prominence — he was Julius Schmahl,

former state treasurer. To many local residents, it seemed smart to invest their money with the likes of Burnquist and Schmahl.

The two men and several of their Republican colleagues founded Modern Life Insurance Company in 1921 in a fifth-floor office of the Endicott Building at Fourth and Robert streets. In fact, for more than 50 years, the insurance company has been a Fourth Street resident — first in the Endicott Building, then in a Grecian-styled showcase on Fourth and Minnesota and then — when growth demanded yet another company move — to Fourth and Wall streets. By early 1980, The North Central Companies expect to occupy several floors in a 25-story twin tower office complex planned for the block between Seventh and Eighth streets and Minnesota and Cedar streets in the center of St. Paul's new Seventh Place redevelopment area.

In the early years, the Modern Life insurance firm confined its business to Minnesota with standard policies and relatively conservative ways. Employees and the company's founders were a congenial group who frequently spent their leisure time together in summer outings on Leech Lake.

C

A   *The planned NORTH CENTRAL LIFE Tower, new headquarters building in the Seventh Place redevelopment area*
B   *The "little Greek temple" which was North Central's home from 1958 to 1966*
C   *Proudly displaying his derby, founder J.A.A. Burnquist rides in the Armistice Day parade as Minnesota governor*

There, Julius Schmahl, an amateur historian, delivered lectures on state history and led campfire sing-a-longs. The company's growth was steady, yet modest in the early years, through the Depression and the Second World War. But in the late Forties, the firm's approach and energy-level changed dramatically with the influence and sales leadership of young Ted Sanborn. In his mid-twenties, Sanborn had begun selling insurance for a rival company in 1946. He proved his expertise by selling more than $700,000 worth of life insurance in his first six months. Sanborn soon left that rival firm and joined Modern Life. He quickly began to take home commissions and earnings greater than the salary of Modern Life's president! With that show of personal promise, Sanborn was promoted to the firm's home office in St. Paul and named Director of Agencies. By 1951, Sanborn and a group of his friends and associates bought controlling interest in the insurance company and, at 29, Sanborn became the youngest president of any North American insurance company. He changed the Modern Life name to North Central Life and diversified the firm's services to include life and disability insurance for installment loans. That market was virtually untapped in Minnesota and the pioneering credit insurance division of North Central Life grew swiftly. By 1962, the division was selling credit insurance through more Upper Midwest financial institutions than all other life companies combined.

The new service touched many people in Minnesota because it made credit insurance available for such things as auto, home and business loans. Young Minnesota businessmen looked to North Central for help in covering such wide-ranging expenditures as buying new cars, whole new businesses, feeder cattle for farms, or new truck-trailer rigs for fledgling transport firms.

North Central grew dramatically. Among its diversified services, it had more than $100 million worth of life insurance in force by 1960, and the firm ranked in the top 18 percent of all life companies in the country. That same year, the firm "went public" and created the financial holding company called The North Central Companies, Inc., with North Central Life as its first and principal subsidiary.

Today, North Central Life currently has more than 1,000 financial institutions as customers, insures nearly 400,000 people, is licensed to do business in 40 states, and ranks in the top 15 percent of life insurance companies in premium income. Three times since 1951, the company ranked as the fastest-growing life insurance company in the United States according to industry sources.

By mid-1977, the firm had nearly $1.5 billion worth of insurance in force.

Coincidentally, Ted Sanborn celebrated his 50th birthday on the 50th anniversary of his firm in 1971. He is a member of a long established St. Paul family and he feels a strong allegiance to the city. In earlier years, Sanborn's decision to locate his insurance business in St. Paul demonstrated his hope for revitalization of that downtown area. In that historical context, Sanborn's involvement in St. Paul's new redevelopment area, today, seems quite appropriate.

223

Northern Malleable Iron Company

A

Northern Malleable Iron Co. had a corner on the market from the very beginning. When the company was founded in 1905, it was the only one of its kind in Minnesota. It remains so today.

At first, Northern Malleable found most of its business with farmers and railroad men. Rural customers needed malleable iron parts of all kinds for their horse-drawn wagons and crude farm machinery. Nine railroad operations converging in St. Paul created a healthy demand for castings in the construction of tracks and railroad cars. The future of Northern Malleable was promising in those days, especially with the leadership of such well-known people as agri-business wizards Charles Deering and Cyrus McCormick, businessman Frank J. Ottis, Attorney C.A. Severance, and statesman Frank B. Kellogg.

Soon after incorporation, Northern Malleable moved to its current production site on the Eastside of St. Paul and set to work producing approximately 4,500 tons of castings yearly. Although some single castings weighed as much as 200 pounds, the average casting was less than a pound. Much work was done by hand in the rambling production plant at Forest and Wells with melting done in hand fired, coal burning furnaces. Women were well-accepted members of the work-force. They were among a large number of immigrants from Poland, Sweden, Italy, Rumania and Germany. In fact, the 1906 edition of employee rules and regulations at Northern Malleable was printed in at least seven languages.

Today, the tough, resilient malleable iron that was a mainstay of the company's business in the early years has been supplanted by "ductile iron," a

material with different strength properties demanded by a whole new breed of customers. Today, Northern Malleable can produce about 16,000 tons of castings per year for manufacturers of trucks, auto parts, construction equipment vehicles and sophisticated farm machinery. Annual business totals approximately $10 million. Along with producing castings for the complex crop harvesters and gadabout all-terrain vehicles of our modern society, however, Northern Malleable still makes at least 10,000 castings for wringer washers each month. Instead of coal-fired furnaces, the firm now utilizes more than two million kilowatt hours of electricity monthly for melting iron in their electric induction furnaces and operating the highly mechanized equipment.

Donald Fulton, whose father served as President of Northern Malleable nearly 30 years ago, is now President of the firm. He says one approach to the business certainly has not changed over the years: "We were recycling materials long before the term was fashionable. From the beginning, Northern Malleable's main source of raw material has been scrap metal, first iron and now steel. Given the production process, the same pound of scrap can be recycled many times over."

A   *Women were a major portion of work force in 1910.*
B   *Thousands of malleable castings await early farm and railroad customers*

B

North Star Steel Company

North Star Steel Company, the Northwest's only steel mill, was founded in 1965 as a joint venture of Canadian and Twin City business interests. The two individuals primarily responsible for the venture were Canadian G.R. Heffernan, who had built and operated two successful steel mills in Canada, and J.B. Klemp, a former F.B.I. agent but no stranger to the steel business.

The two men chose their new business site — 200 acres in the St. Paul Port Authority Industrial Park — and soon became interwoven in the city's history. Klemp learned that Indians who once roamed the Mississippi River bluffs called the acreage "Red Rock." Their tribal landmark was a huge rock positioned nearby. For years, the rock was a symbolic focal point for victorious war parties (the red color, Klemp later learned, represented the blood of unlucky victims). With an eye on history, Klemp and his colleague convinced the Port Authority to rename acreage that was to be the first home for North Star Steel, the Red Rock Industrial Park.

Today, North Star is a wholly-owned subsidiary of Cargill, a private company with roots leading back to Minnesota's territorial days.

North Star's "continuous casting" method of producing steel has eliminated one major step in the production line and permits the company's facilities to be smaller than most, yet more efficient. North Star currently ships about 400,000 tons of finished steel products annually to customers all over the country, and, with the completion of current expansion, will increase capacity to 580,000 tons per year. Along with the major plant in St. Paul, North Star also has facilities in Iowa and Duluth, Minnesota. In total, North Star employs nearly 1,000 persons, with 650 working in St. Paul. The company's customers are nationwide, but several major ones are located in St. Paul.

Sales for North Star Steel now exceed $100 million yearly, and represent a substantial advance from 1965 when North Star was just an idea in the minds of two ambitious businessmen.

A

B

C

A *North Star's present facility*
B *Capacity will increase to 580,000 tons per year*
C *Scrap waiting for reclamation*

Paper, Calmenson & Co.

A

B

C

D

It was a modest beginning — one repeated often in turn-of-the-century St. Paul. Lewis Paper and Moses Calmenson opened for business on the east side of St. Paul, close to the railroad tracks, high on hopes and short on office amenities. Included in Paper, Calmenson & Co.'s first business inventory for 1891 were "two wheelbarrows, three hand trucks, one railroad scale, one bale press, two stoves, a safe and a desk".

During those early years, the two businessmen showed characteristic conservatism: "The general nature of our business," they wrote, "shall be in the dealing, buying and vending, at wholesale and retail, of scrap iron, machinery and metals".

In 1905 the Company incorporated, and Lewis Paper became its first president. As time passed, he acquired sole ownership of the business.

It was frequently necessary for Lewis Paper to travel to Chicago on business. On one occasion he became ill just prior to departure. It was his son, Joseph, then only 13 years old, who made that Chicago trip, and acted on behalf of his father.

In 1924 Joseph Paper became the Company's president, and later, his younger brother, David Paper, became vice president. Under the direction of these second generation Papers, the firm diversified widely and grew to be one of the largest family-owned businesses of its kind in the country. Before their deaths, Joseph and David Paper each devoted nearly 50 years to the steel business.

Today, approximately 1000 people are employed at Paper, Calmenson's main office and plant in St. Paul and at its branch manufacturing facility in La Crosse, Wisconsin. The Company's products are marketed under the PACAL trade name. They include a wide range of carbon and alloy steel mill products, industrial steel parts and subassemblies, and a full line of steel blades and accessories for earth-moving and snow removal equipment. The firm is a leading fabricator of structural steel, reinforcing steel, and steel joists and deck for construction projects, and is a major broker of iron and steel scrap for mills and foundries. PACAL products are distributed nationally and throughout Canada.

Paper, Calmenson & Co. continues to be wholly owned by the descendents of its founder, Lewis Paper. In addition to their business interests, the Paper family has long been involved in civic and philanthropic activities. In fact there are few volunteer boards in the area on which a family member has not served.

E

A   *Lewis Paper*
B   *The old plant*
C   *Joseph Paper*
D   *David Paper*
E   *Paper, Calmenson & Co.'s main office and plant, Hwy. 280 at Hwy. 36, St. Paul, Minnesota.*

Plastics, Inc.

A

A   *Paul K. Schilling*

Even in the midst of the Great Depression, energetic Saint Paul businessmen had their dreams to pursue. One of them was S.H.A. Young who owned certain business goodwill in the molded products business and was sole owner of Molded Products Company. In July 1939 he decided to expand the company by acquiring additional financial backing. At the same time Mr. Frank W. Fuller, an engineer who had been looking for a place where he could actively engage in production of some kind, and Mr. Augustine G. Langford, a salesman for Northwestern Mutual Life who wished to get into something else, joined forces with Young.

In January 1940 the company was chartered in Minnesota under the name of Plastics, Inc. Officers elected were: President, Frank W. Fuller; Vice President, Augustine G. Langford; Vice President, S.H.A. Young; Secretary-Treasurer, Dorothy M. Munroe. The new company was located at that time at 20 E. Chicago Avenue where it remained until January 1944 when it was moved to its present location at 224 Ryan Avenue.

For a brief period, Plastics, Inc. maintained a small manufacturing facility in Forest Park, Illinois, under the direction of Mr. Young for the purpose of making dispensers for Cameo Cleanser. Shortly after the opening of this operation, Mr. Young resigned and was replaced by Mr. John U.D. Page. This facility did not prove to be profitable and was subsequently closed.

Shortly after the outbreak of WW II, both Fuller and Page, who held Reserve Army commissions as Captains, were recalled to service. Langford was then elected President, and it was through his able leadership that Plastics, Inc. survived during the war years and started its growth pattern which, following Langford's sudden death in 1952, enabled the company to achieve its outstanding eminence in the plastics field under the capable leadership of Paul K. Schilling, a native of Saint Paul. Much credit must be given to Schilling, who bought into the company in 1955, for his entrepreneurship in making Plastics, Inc. a nationally known organization attractive enough to be acquired in 1968 by Anchor Hocking Corporation of Lancaster, Ohio, as a wholly owned subsidiary.

Their first major product was a line of toilet seats for the Sperzel Company, followed shortly by a line of plastic dishware for Northwest Airlines, Inc. and subsequently for most of the major airlines not only in the U.S. but in the world. Schilling was also the inventor of the disposable plastic glass which is now so commonly used by major institutions such as hotels/motels, airlines, and even for home entertaining of all kinds.

In addition to the continuing manufacture of disposable drinkware and dinnerware, other major products being produced today by Plastics, Inc. are plastic streetlight globes made from a special heat-resistant material and a new revolutionary hot-cold food-service system being marketed by Anchor Hocking Corporation under the name ALPHA® Food Service System. The newest innovation is a line of MICROWARE® products designed particularly for use in microwave ovens but which also have the added advantage of use in conventional gas and electric ovens.

Today, Plastics, Inc. reports sales of approximately $18 million annually, and their headquarters is still located in the same downtown Saint Paul building it first occupied decades ago. Theodore C. Widder, Jr., a specialist in plastics, packaging, and textiles, is the current President of the Saint Paul company.

Saint Paul Area Chamber of Commerce

A

A *Sectional view of the Saint Paul Chamber of Commerce during one of its regular weekly sessions, February, 1898. (Photo by E.R. Shepard — Courtesy, Saint Paul Public Library and Ronald H. Geller.)*

From the very beginning, Saint Paul boosters were a proud lot. With characteristic drama, the Honorable Charles E. Flandreau told members of the fledgling Saint Paul Chamber of Commerce in 1888, "'Twas said, 'All roads lead to Rome.' Today, we bring the saying home. There's not a railroad great or small that does not have its centre in Saint Paul."

The judge was right. Saint Paul was the burgeoning business center of territorial Minnesota in the mid-1800s. Traders navigated the Mississippi River, carying their goods to Saint Paul ports. Railroad men laid miles of tracks leading to the city. Business buildings appeared one by one in downtown Saint Paul, and workmen busied themselves pouring sidewalks, grading streets, installing sewers and hanging cable lines. The city flowed with new business. There were real fortunes to be made.

But what the city needed — along with the ambitious entrepreneurs — was an organization designed to create harmony amidst the activity. So a group of business people, who seemed to care as much about the growth of their city as they did about the expansion of their own enterprises, did just that. They organized the Saint Paul Chamber of Commerce. The alliance of business people actually had many names from its beginning in 1867. For a time, it was the Saint Paul Board of Trade, then the Saint Paul Commercial Club and finally, in 1960, the Saint Paul Area Chamber of Commerce. J.C. Burbank, stagecoach king, politician and connoisseur of the arts, was selected to lead the original Chamber.

Burbank's leadership has been taken up by a diverse group over the years, including retailers, manufacturers, engineers, bankers, wholesalers and professional people.

Today, the Saint Paul Chamber is recognized as one of the leading organizations of its kind in the country. It was, in fact, a first-year charter member of the United States Chamber of Commerce when that organization was formed 65 years ago.

Since its beginning, the Saint Paul Chamber has been committed to maintaining and enhancing the economic well-being of their Capital City. Clearly, one way to achieve that has been to keep existing businesses strong and to attract other major companies to Saint Paul. The Chamber has been instrumental in doing just that on many occasions — and among the most notable examples involved locating the Ford Manufacturing Plant in Highland Park. In addition, Northwest Airlines, a highly successful commercial carrier, had its start thanks to Col. L.H. Brittin, Vice President of the Saint Paul Association (a forerunner of the Saint Paul Area Chamber of Commerce).

Along with a concern for local business development, the Chamber has also demonstrated strong support for the educational, cultural, recreational and social programs that are a vital part of Saint Paul.

Certainly, current members of the Saint Paul Chamber may not swallow that old, grandiose "all roads lead to Rome" philosophy once articulated by Judge Flandreau . . . but they are solidly committed to making Saint Paul the best city it can realistically be.

St. Paul Pioneer Press and Dispatch

On a raw day late in April, 1849, James M. Goodhue stepped ashore from a river steamboat, set up his hand press in the only vacant space in a sprawling hamlet called St. Paul and Minnesota's first newspaper was born.

That weekly newspaper, "The Minnesota Pioneer," was the forerunner of today's St. Paul Pioneer Press, published continuously since 1849.

Goodhue's presence was clearly felt in the early days of St. Paul. He wrote with pride about the advantages of Minnesota and enticed many settlers from the East and South to the region.

In true editorial style, he spoke with vigor on a number of local topics and he was not always congratulated for his opinions — on one occasion, in fact, his editorial stance led to a street duel.

With Goodhue's death in 1852 (just six years before Minnesota was admitted to the union), Joseph B. Brown, a pioneer explorer, township developer, lumberman and politician, became editor of the newspaper. Both men are well-remembered today because two Minnesota counties — Goodhue and Brown — are named in their honor.

Over time, consolidation occurred in the newspaper business. There were plenty of rival publications operating in those days and strength equated with size. So in 1875, Joseph A. Wheelock and Frederick Driscoll, publishers of the St. Paul "Daily Press," bought the Minnesota Pioneer and created what is known today as the St. Paul Pioneer Press. Later, George Thompson, owner of another competing newspaper called the St. Paul Dispatch, bought the Pioneer Press in 1909. With that merger, the Press continued as the morning edition — and the Dispatch brought news of the day to St. Paul homes each evening.

Management changed in 1927 when three Ridder brothers — Bernard, Joseph and Victor — all from New York, bought the two newspapers. Since then, the Ridder interests have expanded to include a group of newspapers in many cities of the country. Today's St. Paul Pioneer Press and Dispatch has a circulation of more than 200,000 and employs about 900 people (another 3,000 are carrier-salespeople). The newspapers were the first in the state to use photocomposition and computer typesetting, and in July, 1977, they became the first Twin Cities newspapers to use a new process of direct photo polymer plate printing on the big, thundering presses.

Old James Goodhue would be proud to see that his instinct for reliable news, quickly conveyed, has reached such technological heights.

A

B   C

D   E

F

A   *James M. Goodhue*
B/E   *Early rivals, the Pioneer and Daily Press were adjacent, then merged*
F   *The St. Paul Dispatch printed facsimile of Declaration of Independence in July 4, 1876, parade*

The St. Paul Companies

The St. Paul Companies, Inc. (originally known as St. Paul Fire and Marine), was founded in 1853 — four years after Minnesota became a territory and five years before statehood.

St. Paul had about 2,500 pioneering citizens when 17 business leaders organized St. Paul Fire and Marine Insurance Company. It was the era of Red River ox carts, Indian trade and river boats . . . and the trade, in particular, demanded insurance protection. Appropriately, the founders of St. Paul Fire and Marine focused their efforts on providing insurance against fire damage and what they so politely described as "the perils of marine and inland navigation." Capt. Alexander Wilkin was the company's first president. A slight man, just five feet tall and 100 pounds, Wilkin soon became known as "Little Captain" to Minnesotans (Wilkin was, however, small in stature only. In time, he owned half of downtown St. Paul). Other officers of St. Paul Fire and Marine also were Minnesota notables — including George Farrington, the first secretary of the company, who was a member of the St. Paul City Council and the Territorial Legislature, and William Pitt Murray, company vice president, who served in the legislature (Murray County was named after him).

During the company's first year in operation, $380.40 in premiums for fire and marine protection were paid. Three years later, the pioneer corporation had already recorded the sale of 203 policies.

Business was minimal during the Civil War, but, as the war drew to a close, the country's economy expanded and so did activity for the St. Paul-based company. St. Paul Fire and Marine's new president, James C. Burbank, was a man with substantial connections in Canada and he established the company's first international business there in 1865. The firm's first recorded entry into St. Paul civic affairs also occurred during that year when St. Paul Fire and Marine loaned the city $2,500 to buy a steam fire engine. And, in 1870, the firm invested $66,000 in a headquarters building at Third and Jackson streets. The building was lauded as a "splendid and elegant" addition to the downtown area.

Over the years, St. Paul Fire and Marine expanded its insurance offerings and managed to survive major catastrophies that put many other companies out of business. The Great Chicago Fire of 1871 was the first challenge. St. Paul Fire and Marine was faced with $142,000 in claims from that fire. Those losses amounted to 165% more than all of its sales in the nation in 1870. President James Burbank personally went to Chicago to supervise the settlements. All losses were paid within three

A

months. Shareholders in St. Paul Fire and Marine received no dividends that year, but the company recovered from that historic disaster with remarkable resilience. In July, 1872, dividend payments were resumed and were never interrupted again.

Trouble struck again in 1906 when the worst fire in history burned San Francisco. Until Hurricane Betsy slashed the southern United States almost 60 years later, the San Francisco fire and earthquake caused the largest single insurance loss ever, nearly $164 million. Once again, St. Paul Fire and Marine paid its claims in full — a total of $1,267,000. The amount was about equal to the company's total capital and surplus at the time.

World War I was no small challenge, either. Because St. Paul Fire and Marine offered extensive ocean marine insurance by that time, the loss payments on 260 wartime vessels were significant.

Over nearly 125 years, in fact, St. Paul Fire and Marine proved to be rock-solid. Even during the Depression, recession, bank failures, wars and natural catastrophies.

Today, The St. Paul Companies deal not only with insurance of many kinds — property, liability, life, health and title — but also consumer finance, investment banking, leasing and mutual funds. Its subsidiaries now include Western Life and St. Paul

Life Insurance Companies, St. Paul Title Insurance Corporation, Postal Finance Co., John Nuveen & Co., Inc., St. Paul Advisers, Inc., and The St. Paul Leasing Co. The non-insurance subsidiaries were acquired in the past decade.

In 1968, St. Paul Fire and Marine Insurance Company was officially changed to a management company and given its new name, The St. Paul Companies, Inc. In Fortune Magazine's most recent list of the 50 largest diversified financial companies, the firm was ranked 20th in assets and 11th in revenues. The St. Paul Companies has become a $2-1/2 billion enterprise led by C.B. Drake, Jr., President and Chief Executive Officer. There are nearly 8,500 employees throughout the U.S. and Canada, and the insurance premiums that once totaled $380.40 now exceed $1 billion annually.

A   *First St. Paul Companies building, Third and Jackson streets*
B   *Territorial Governor Ramsey's letter approving company incorporation*
C   *Oldest policy on file provided $500 fire coverage against $5 annual premium*

B

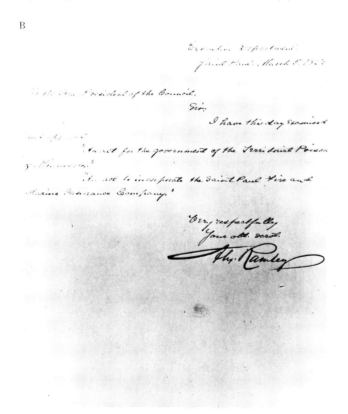

C

St. Paul Union Stockyards

Why transport 75,000 Western cattle through St. Paul to Chicago, and then watch 75,000 beef carcasses, plus sides of pork and lamb, come back from Chicago to satisfy the appetites of St. Paul residents?

It appeared to A.B. Stickney, president of the Minnesota and Northwestern Railroad, the system could be improved. With that conviction, Stickney invited a few St. Paul businessmen, Western cattlemen and railroad officials to meet with him at the Minnesota Club in May, 1886. Stickney quickly convinced his colleagues that St. Paul could establish its own livestock market and meat packing center and effectively eliminate that 800-mile round trip to Chicago. Stickney also envisioned the gaunt range cattle of the West growing fat on the abundant pastures and feed grains offered by a number of Twin City area farmers.

Stickney had broad-based support for his plan, but a notable backer was railroad "empire builder" James J. Hill, who was already in the business of growing and feeding livestock at his North Oaks estate. With the help of Hill's advocacy, a cash commitment was made, a lowland site along the banks of the Mississippi River was selected, construction began, and the first trainload of livestock arrived at the South St. Paul stockyards on September 30, 1887. The cargo included seven loads of Washington State steers consigned by a Scotsman named Ramsey.

From these idealistic beginnings, the St. Paul Union Stockyards did indeed grow and develop according to the expectations of A.B. Stickney.

The millionth head of livestock arrived at South St. Paul in 1889, just two years after the market opened. By 1901 ten million head were counted, by 1946 200 million, and in 1965 the 300 millionth head of livestock was marketed at what had become one of America's dominant public markets.

But Stickney's projections were not fully realized until 1974 when the South St. Paul stockyard marketed over 3-1/4 million head of livestock worth over $550 million and was officially proclaimed "The Largest Livestock Market in the World."

In 1977, still the Largest in the World, the St. Paul Union Stockyards demonstrated its continued commitment to its growth and dominance of the livestock industry in the form of a new 1.5-million-dollar office building. Constructed in a Western motif using rough sawn cedar and old stockyard paving bricks, this building will serve the industry as its new trade center.

Even though "St. Paul '77" is primarily urban, a day's activities at the St. Paul Union Stockyards still offers a glimpse of the Old West and pioneering St. Paul.

A   *The original stockyards Exchange Building — built in 1887.*

B   *The new $1.5 million South St. Paul Exchange Building — 1977.*

A

B

Shaw Lumber Co.

The Shaw family of Minnesota is approaching five generations in the lumber business, and its history is rooted in the era of the pioneers who developed the once-thriving timber industry of the Northern Minnesota forest areas. George S. Shaw was the family trend-setter when in the 1880's, he went to Cloquet, Minn., to take over management of a small lumber mill. This became the Cloquet Lumber Co. which grew to be one of the major timber processors of its day.

At the same time, his eldest son, Willis R. Shaw, who had been associated in the building business in Davenport with his father, moved to St. Paul and in 1886 opened a retail lumber yard at State and Concord Streets. When the livestock industry came to South St. Paul, he moved his yard there to take advantage of the building growth that the packing plants brought with them. After his death in 1909, the business was carried on by his son, Louis F. Shaw and son-in-law Z.H. Hutchinson. To better serve the growing metropolitan area of St. Paul, yards were established in West St. Paul and on Como Avenue in St. Paul during the 1920s.

After World War II, the next generation of the Shaw family assumed control, with George Shaw Withy as president and John T. Withy as secretary-treasurer ... both grandsons of Willis Shaw. With George Withy as the active family member in the business, the South St. Paul yard was "retired," and the company's main office was moved to 217 Como Avenue in St. Paul. A new yard in Arden Hills was acquired to serve the growing northern suburbs, and the company set out to become a true "full service" building materials supplier to the construction trade of the Twin Cities.

Although Shaw Lumber for many years had been in the millwork business in addition to its lumber trade, this was expanded with a new plant and new machinery, enabling the company to compete over the entire region in cabinet work, architectural millwork, and specialty milling of hardwood lumber, door and window units and mouldings. Schools, churches and major buildings, as well as many fine residences throughout the Twin Cities, have millwork from Shaw's.

In 1970 the decision was made to go into the building component business — the fabrication of roof and floor truss systems, wall panels, and the revolutionary all-weather wood foundation system, introduced to Minnesota by Shaw's. This occasioned the construction of another plant for this purpose at the Como Avenue headquarters, close to the yard supplies and the main office. In addition, the company did not forget the home-owner, establishing well-stocked retail departments at each yard to cater to his building and remodelling needs. Thus came the term, "full-service" dealer.

Today Shaw's lumber products come in only limited quantities from northern Minnesota, instead being shipped here mainly from the west and south. But the pioneering spirit of the Shaw name still prevails, as this innovative company continues to seek out new ways and products to better serve its growing list of customers.

A

A   *Shaw's yard in South St. Paul, early 1900's.*

J. L. Shiely Company

A

B

J.L. Shiely, Sr., had an early introduction to the construction industry. In 1898, when Shiely was 14, this son of a St. Paul teaming contractor worked summers for a major St. Paul construction firm. In the early years, the young boy helped build the Minnesota State Capitol, the St. Paul Public Library and the Minnesota Club — all coveted projects of his first employers.

From that time, J.L. Shiely never left the construction business. He worked on the Iron Range and on railroad projects in Minnesota, North

Dakota and Montana (later he was stationed in Helena, Montana, supervising construction of a new depot). Shiely ultimately became a clerk, assistant engineer, roadmaster and inspector for the Great Northern Railway Engineering Department.

By 1912, J.L. Shiely decided it was time to leave the railroad and go into business for himself. Grant Smith, a railroad contractor, who later built the Burlington-Northern, Inc. headquarters building at 5th & Jackson, St. Paul recommended Shiely to S.J. Groves and Sons Co., then building the Dan Patch Line (MN&S). This led to an association with C.C. "Blackie" Smith who suggested that Shiely go in the sand and gravel business in St. Paul. Shiely joined in partnership with Smith, and the two each put up $1,000 for their enterprise. Within two years, the partnership had paid for all the teams, wagons, horses and materials they required to start their fledgling business. Later, in 1914 Shiely bought his partner out for $10,000. He was then joined by Daniel L. Bell, a wealthy St. Paul building materials dealer, and the J.L. Shiely Company was incorporated. The company built the first fixed crushing, washing and screening plant for the production of construction aggregate in the Twin Cities. It was located on the west side of Dale Street in St. Paul. By 1919, the senior Shiely was joined by his brother, Albert, who had just earned a law degree and completed overseas service in World War I. Another brother, James Martin Shiely, joined the company in 1929. The company's family lineage has never been broken. J.L. Shiely, Jr. is still Chairman of the Board and Chief Executive Officer of this long-time St. Paul enterprise. Company president is Donald C. Reioux.

Today, although the firm was involved in a number of construction-related fields over its long history, it has now focused on providing ready-mixed concrete and aggregate for the Twin Cities metropolitan area construction industry. J.L. Shiely Company has produced basic materials for most of the major construction projects and buildings in the St. Paul-Minneapolis area. The company has an operation in St. Cloud, Minnesota, and two in Denver, Colorado.

A   *The christening of Joe Al Jim II*
B   *Initial voyage*

234

H.M. Smyth Printing Company, Inc.

How proud the printers of St. Paul were in the early 1900's. H.M. Smyth Printing Company produced a full-color booklet featuring a two-page drawing of their "new, modern, sanitary building with daylight streaming in on three sides" at Ninth and Temperance streets in St. Paul. And with justifiable pride, the owners boasted: "This entire building is owned and occupied exclusively by us."

A

B

Even then, the Smyth printing firm enjoyed seniority in downtown St. Paul. The company's handsome founder, H.M. Smyth, began printing business cards, small folders, letterheads and invoices for St. Paul clients as early as 1877. Business was not easy to come by in those days, but H.M. Smyth Printing expanded steadily and outgrew two offices in the first 14 years. It seems Smyth people were particularly innovative. F.H. Warwich, one of the founder's loyal successors, for example, came to be known as St. Paul's "father of lithography" when the printing firm became the first west of Chicago to use that new technique. In fact, most of H.M. Smyth's successors had printer's ink and printer's enterprise surging through their

veins. G.G. (Mac) McGuiggan — president of Smyth in the early 1900's — started work as a boy in the offices of a rival printing company. He later became the Smyth shop foreman and soon rocketed to President, Treasurer and General Manager (roles he held at the same time). Current President and Chairman of the Board, William J. Hickey, Jr., is McGuiggan's grandson. The junior Hickey followed his father in H.M. Smyth's corporate chain of command and, today, the Hickey family counts more than 80 years in the St. Paul printing business. Instead of calling cards and letterheads, however, H.M. Smyth now prints millions of labels, consumer packages and point-of-purchase displays for the likes of Green Giant, Hormel, Armour, Libby, Gillette, Borden, General Mills and Pillsbury. The firm designs colorful packaging for everything from canned corn to crepe pans to parakeet food, and some are printed in foreign languages for multinational corporations. H.M. Smyth also designs and prints many annual reports for firms in the Ninth Federal Reserve District and designs catalogs and advertising pieces for many Twin Cities companies. The firm moved to its current St. Paul site on North Snelling Avenue 21 years ago and invested heavily in new printing equipment. But even with noteworthy business growth in the past two decades, William Hickey Senior and Junior remained visibly involved in civic affairs. The company's management has always encouraged employee involvement in such activities.

Most recently, the junior Hickey was named St. Paul's "Boss of the Year" for 1976 — an honor that even the modest printing President is happy to mention.

A *Early office*
B *Smyth's first plant on northwest corner of Kellogg Blvd. and Cedar St.*

Space Center

St. Paul warehousemen of the early 1900's had a valuable service to sell. Freight cars loaded with goods were transported into the city for local distribution, and once unloaded, the agricultural chemicals, the nails, the shingles, logs and Model T cars required storage somewhere, and one likely spot was the St. Paul Terminal Warehouse Company, a 300,000-square-foot facility on Lafayette Avenue, operated by H.G. McNeely, Sr. It was particularly convenient because it was near the Mississippi River and railroads traditionally travel alongside level river beds. Knowing that demands for storage space could only increase as St. Paul and its neighbor Minneapolis grew, McNeely opened a similar warehouse in Minneapolis and several other locations throughout the Twin Cities. As a natural adjunct to warehousing, local delivery service was developed, and many a "four-foot fleet" of dray wagons could be seen picking up and delivering supplies for local merchants.

Today, SPACE CENTER, Inc., the successor name to St. Paul and Minneapolis Terminal Warehouse Company, has enlarged its expansive commodity to include three and a half million square feet at eleven locations in the Twin Cities, two million square feet in Ontario, California, two million square feet in Warren, Ohio, one and a half million square feet in Kansas City, Missouri, one half million square feet in Quincy, Illinois, and one million square feet in Dallas, Texas. The space in Kansas City and Quincy, by the way, is totally underground, having taken advantage of vacated limestone mines. Temperature and humidity are controlled for quality assurance of all products.

In addition to its warehousing activities, SPACE CENTER, Inc., has expanded its horse-and-wagon transportation service of the 1900's to more than 1,200 trucks rolling to destinations all over the central United States from Minnesota to Texas and from Colorado to Ohio.

Along with these services, the firm is involved in Collateral Financial Services as a nation-wide business. In brief, warehouse receipts are issued on the site of the manufacturer for merchandise stored and used as security for bank borrowings. Along with bank participation lease programs and a variety of financial services, SPACE CENTER, Inc., is truly the most versatile physical distribution service company in the United States. Although many of its customers are Fortune "500"

enterprises, it has not forgotten that its roots started with the smaller growth company who needed service to satisfy his customer's customer demand.

Today, logistic services are in more demand than ever before. Distributors, suppliers, jobbers and manufacturers who once settled for mail-order delivery and the inevitable long order cycle time before receipt, now expect immediate delivery of every product size, color and model imaginable. At SPACE CENTER, Inc., the objective is not only to meet, but to exceed the needs and demands of its customers.

A *Horse and wagons, trains, and trucks were all used at Space Center's warehouse, known in 1918 as St. Paul Terminal Warehouse Co.*
B *Warehouse as it appears today (1978).*

A

B

Sperry Univac Division of
Sperry Rand Corporation

A

Just after World War II, a handful of ex-Navy scientists put their heads together in Minnesota and started a company called ERA — Engineering Research Associates, Inc. These men were short on cash and equipment but long on vision and hope. The original 39 employees moved into a cavernous building on West Minnehaha Avenue, a former production site for World War II plywood gliders, and found it to be a lonely setting: "There were more sparrows than people inside," one employee remembers.

The production staff immediately set to work making such unrelated items as gasporters and bore-hole cameras to keep money coming in, while the ERA scientists tackled their primary interests — digital computers, magnetic storage and data handling systems.

That same year, across the country in Philadelphia, J. Presper Eckert and John Mauchly began a series of experiments in the basement of the engineering school at the University of Pennsylvania. The pair had been assigned by the U.S. Army to devise a computing device. With a staggering array of vacuum tubes, wires and switches, Eckert and Mauchly created ENIAC, the first general purpose electronic calculator weighing no less than 30 tons and occupying a floor area of more than 300 square feet. ENIAC was, however, capable of managing an incredible 4,500 computations per second.

The achievements of Eckert and Mauchly and ERA in those early years soon caught the eye of Remington Rand, Inc., and together these computer pioneers formed what today is Sperry Univac, a division of Sperry Rand Corporation. (The actual term Univac, was coined by Eckert and Mauchly. It means Universal Automatic Computer).

From the company's beginning in 1946, the largest concentration of Sperry Univac staff people has been in Minnesota, with a majority in the St. Paul area. Multiple plant sites include Roseville (where most of the large-scale Sperry Univac computers are developed and made), the Midway area (the original office site, now assigned to computer testing and support), Eagan (headquarters for the Sperry Univac defense systems division) and Shepard Road. The original computer firm in Minnesota in its first 30 years grew to approximately 10,000 employees, with about 9,500 of them in these St. Paul facilities. Sperry Univac's worldwide products sales also was generating annual computer-related revenues of nearly $1.5 billion by 1976.

Today's computers weigh significantly less and demand a fraction of the space and energy required by the ponderous initial devices. There are portable computer terminals no bigger than a standard briefcase, and computers available even for home use. Instead of the 4,500 computations per second that so impressed people in 1946, computers today can now easily handle 15 to 20 million computations each second. What seemed like science fiction before is clearly reality now. And the future lies ahead.

A   *UNIVAC 1103 computer (1954)*

Standard Conveyor Company

A

Some jobs are meant to be mechanized. That certainly applied to carrying bulky bundles of cedar shingles arriving by the carload at a lumber yard in the Midway district of St. Paul. Charlie Lister was particularly sensitive about shingles because he was assigned to lug them from the boxcar to storage sheds.

In the early 1900's, no one had devised a better method to handle the mundane task. So Charlie did. He nailed the round tops of baking powder tins to narrow wooden 2x4" stringers and mounted them together in pairs. He propped the pairs up and discovered that the simple force of gravity carried a bundle of shingles quite nicely from the boxcar to the shed. A modest invention, wheel conveyor, yet one that by 1906 set the conveyor industry in real motion.

From 1906 on, this concept of a simple gravity wheel conveyor was broadened with the innovative efforts of Lister and W.S. McCurdy to include the development of gravity roller conveyor, spiral chutes, spiral roller conveyors, and many types of powered conveyors. Today the same company, started by Lister and McCurdy, expanded and developed under Harry L. Donahower for 43 years, is in its 72nd year producing complex conveying systems, as well as the original gravity wheel conveyor.

The Standard Conveyor Company is still at the original pastoral location selected early in its corporate life as an ideal spot for a manufacturing facility, with good rail and road connections, reliable public transportation (streetcars) and a skilled labor pool in an ideal suburban living area.

John Donahower, who joined the firm more than 44 years ago as an accountant and blueprint "expert," is now president and chief executive officer. The company is one of few closely-held family companies remaining in the materials handling industry. Standard Conveyor sales in a single year now approach $18 million — quite a change from the days when Charlie Lister found his fortune in baking powder tin covers and 2x4 rails.

B

C

A   *Powered chain "piler" conveyor carrying bagged coffee. Used in Brazil about 1925.*
B   *Computer controlled, modern pallet conveyors for feeding automated storage system.*
C   *Standard roller conveyor in 1918 version of a shipping department.*

Standard Conveyor is today an important factor in the materials handling industry, specializing in "custom built" systems for unit handling of many diverse products. The company's extensive engineering staff designs equipment and develops solutions to conveying problems for many of the major firms in the United States and Canada. The "custom built" concept of Standard's major products still includes gravity wheel conveyor, a viable product in the marketplace after 72 years.

TapeMark

A

A *TapeMark Manufacturing Plant*

A century ago, consumers in St. Paul had little need for printed labels on their products, for decorative designs on their recreational vehicles and for pressure-sensitive bandages for their wounds.

But times have changed dramatically and a number of new St. Paul companies have emerged to satisfy the specialized needs of this sophisticated age. One of those companies is TapeMark of West St. Paul, a firm that originated in 1950 with the express purpose of printing words, colors and designs on pressure-sensitive tape produced by another, not-so-small company in St. Paul called 3M.

TapeMark opened its first office in downtown St. Paul and — with that start — became one of the first companies in the world to print on pressure-sensitive tapes. It has been an innovator in the industry since then. Originally pressure-sensitive tapes were used mainly for advertising, for instructive labels and for identification. TapeMark has gone far beyond that, however. Today, the firm makes countless labels for consumer food companies and also novelty labels.

The firm has designed a series of improved pressure-sensitive adhesive pads for electrocardiogram tests, stress tests and other measurements of the body's vital signs; it has produced do-it-yourself kits for children to decorate their toys. TapeMark has even produced pressure-sensitive labels for space exploration equipment sent to the moon. Today, the firm has equipment that can print pressure-sensitive labels in as many as five colors and apply labels at the rate of more than 1,000 a minute.

Since the Fifties, TapeMark's staff has grown from one person to 200 people and the small office downtown has been traded for two, large buildings covering approximately 85,000 square feet just east of Robert Street. The firm plans to add a third building that will supply another 35,000 square feet of work space soon.

Although TapeMark's major market is concentrated in the five-state Midwest area, it has clients all over the country.

TapeMark President Robert Klas has been a St. Paul resident for some time and has become involved with the children of the city in an important way as originator of the TapeMark Charity Pro-Am Golf Tournament. The annual event was created to benefit retarded children and adults and in the first six years, the tournament has raised $236,000 for retarded citizens of St. Paul.

3M Company

3M Headquarters, nerve center of a $3.6 billion worldwide organization

The 3M Company had a very inauspicious beginning. It was founded in 1902 in Two Harbors, on the north shore of Lake Superior, to mine and sell what was believed to be a valuable raw material for grinding wheel manufacturers. But the mineral turned out to be worthless and in desperation the company was moved to Duluth and began to manufacture sandpaper. Failure continued to plague the company and it was moved again, in 1910, to St. Paul.

Gradually, the company improved the quality of its products and the effectiveness of its salesmanship. New product development and the stimulus of World War I put the company solidly on its feet for the first time. The company paid its first dividend to stockholders in 1916 and has not missed a quarterly payment since that time.

This same year saw still another milestone in the company's development. The sum of $500 was invested in 3M's first laboratory in an effort to improve quality control. Within a few years, laboratory activities were expanded to include new product development, and the 1920's saw the introduction of waterproof sandpaper and "Scotch" masking tape — the forerunner of today's line of more than 600 varieties of pressure sensitive tapes.

These early laboratory activities laid the foundation for what is today a vast research and development program in which 3M has invested more than half a billion dollars in the last five years alone. years alone.

3M today is a $3.6 billion worldwide organization with headquarters in St. Paul. It is the largest private employer in Minnesota with some 20,000 employees in the state.

The company tries to be a good citizen wherever it operates. While its economic presence is most readily recognized, 3M people are also deeply involved in the civic and cultural life of Minnesota as they are in other areas where the company has operations.

Diversifications through the development of new products has been a major factor in 3M's growth and success over the years. The company has 45 major product lines, with 36 U.S. divisions and 10 subsidiaries organized into nine product groups. Major markets include transportation, health care, communications, electronics, education and safety.

Raymond H. Herzog is Chairman and Chief Executive Officer, Lewis W. Lehr is President, U.S. Operations, and James A. Thwaits, President, International Operations.

240

Torit Division of the Donaldson Company

A

B

St. Paul dentists owe much to the Torit Division of Donaldson Company, Inc., a firm based nearly 65 years in St. Paul. In its early days of manufacturing, Torit produced welding gear and, quite by accident, discovered that local dentists needed a small, fine tipped welding torch to do crown and bridge work. Demand enhanced supply and the little company based on the south side of Kellogg Boulevard set to work making tiny welding torches expressly for their new dental clientele. Looking back, that single product led to dozens of other dental items and represents Torit's real entry into big business.

A.E. Swanson, St. Paul native with an acute entrepreneurial eye, provided the leadership for his company's early ventures even though he was just 24 in 1915 when the welding enterprise was founded. During the Depression, while other companies floundered, Swanson offered shares of stock in lieu of wages and managed to keep the company solvent.

By 1938, the company's business course changed, when the company started to market a gadget designed to gather gold dust produced when dentists grind a gold inlay, crown or bridge. Later, this "dust collector" was adapted for companies of all kinds and Torit became a specialist in what later was to become an enterprise devoted exclusively to manufacturing anti-pollution devices. Torit is now considered the leading producer of medium size dust collectors for in-plant use, with national distribution and branches or licensees in six foreign countries.

Today, Torit is a division of Donaldson Company, Inc., another major producer of air cleaning devices based in Minneapolis. Sales for the Torit Division now approach $14 million annually. William West, President of Torit from 1954 to 1974, is a member of the Donaldson Board of Directors and director of the Donaldson Foundation. For West, a St. Paul resident since birth, foundation work is a joy. As chief coordinator of corporate giving, West has much personal experience in local volunteer work. And with Torit's long residence in St. Paul, William West's involvement in the city could be no more appropriate.

A   *Original home of Torit Division, June 1936*
B   *Torit's original 26 employees in 1936*

241

The United States Bedding Company

A

As early as 1898, Samuel Bronstien was sure that the bedding business was no "sleeper." To prove his commitment, young Samuel set up a one-man, one-room mattress factory in his St. Paul home on Tenth Street near the downtown area. There, every mattress was hand-filled, hand-sewn and hand-delivered to customers by Samuel, himself. He was an industrious fellow, often moving his products about town by horse-drawn wagon. It wasn't an easy business, but it was Samuel's own, and he persevered through the building years. Samuel created an impressive line of mattresses, frames, pillows and couches designed for the economy-minded customers of turn-of-the-century St. Paul, as well as for the spendthrifts. In 1912, for example, the finest, curled horse-hair mattress cost a whopping $45, while cotton batting mattresses could be secured for $19 and economy models might cost as little as $5.50. It took years before the traditional hair and cotton-filled mattresses were replaced by wire mesh springs designed to make sleeping easier and more sanitary.

Not one to think small, Samuel Bronstien advanced from a one-man operation to 23 employees and then to 150 in less than 15 years. In 1927, however, Samuel's burgeoning mattress plant burned down in subzero January weather. The 11-alarm fire was considered the worst in St. Paul history, but the tragedy didn't discourage Samuel —

he built a new plant at the current site on Vandalia in the Midway district the same year. Even during the Depression, United States Bedding proved to be a durable survivor. A federal Youth Conservation Corps' order for 25,000 mattresses and, later, massive mattress orders for World War II servicemen helped keep the company afloat.

Today, United States Bedding has expanded to include 10 manufacturing plants and 14 additional licensed manufacturers in the United States and several foreign countries. The company now ranks as the third-largest manufacturer of sleep equipment in America. In a single year, the firm makes nearly two million King Koil and Englander brand mattresses.

Four generations of Bronstiens have been involved in management of this St. Paul company, and today no less than five Bronstiens represent those generations. Consistent family involvement of this kind has been important to United States Bedding over the years. That longevity is dramatically highlighted in 1978 — for in that year, the enterprise marks its 80th anniversary as a St. Paul-based and St. Paul-founded company.

A *The original office of the United States Bedding Company*

242

The Webb Company

Nearly 100 years ago, a young newspaper reporter named Edward A. Webb was covering rural life around Fargo, North Dakota.

As a journalist, Webb saw that coverage of farm

A

A   *The staff of Webb Publishing Company (as it was called until 1973) is shown standing in front of the Webb and The Farmer buildings, at 10th Street and Cedar, about 1912. When Edward Webb moved his operation to St. Paul, he first rented a building on the site of what is now the St. Paul Athletic Club; he later moved to the buildings shown here, which are on the site of what is now the Capitol Square Building facing the State Capitol. With the addition of another building, it was the home of The Webb Company until it moved to its present site in 1962.*

news wasn't what it ought to be. So, in 1882, he purchased a magazine he renamed *The Farmer*. It was written strictly for and about farmers in Minnesota, North Dakota and South Dakota. It was a first in the Midwest and, with Webb single-handedly writing, printing and distributing, was an unchallenged success.

After eight years, as readership grew into the thousands, the energetic publisher, then 38, moved his operation to downtown St. Paul, where he had much better access to timely farming information produced by the University of Minnesota School of Agriculture. It was also close to the Capitol, where Webb was able to exercise his influence on agricultural matters in the state.

The Farmer is still the "flagship" magazine of The Webb Company. Nearly all farmers in Minnesota, North Dakota and South Dakota read *The Farmer* twice monthly except in December; circulation is now about 187,000. However, *The Farmer* has been joined by 10 other magazines published by the company, plus some 13 others written and produced by Webb's creative department for clients throughout the United States, including three inflight magazines for major commercial airlines.

Although agricultural magazines are still the largest revenue producers among the Webb-published magazines, others deal with such diverse topics as canoeing, snowmobiling, and do-it-yourself projects.

In addition to its publishing operation, Webb now has one of the largest printing facilities in the Upper Midwest, with plants both on Shepard Road and in Minneapolis (Midwest Printing Company, a wholly-owned subsidiary). The many large presses print millions of catalogs, telephone directories, brochures and magazines each year.

Edward Webb's one-man operation of 1882 has grown to 1,000 employees, and the small printing press Webb used to put out the early editions of *The Farmer* has grown to $23 million worth of sophisticated modern printing equipment and facilities, with annual sales in 1977 surpassing $70 million.

The Webb Company Board Chairman is Reuel Harmon, whose father was associated with Edward Webb 60 years ago. Harmon is an active St. Paulite who has played a leadership role in the Civic Center and the new zoo in Apple Valley, and has been a strong advocate of downtown redevelopment.

Active head of the company is Robert Haugan, president, who joined Webb as Controller more than 20 years ago, and who is helping maintain The Webb Company's traditional leadership both in the printing and publishing fields, as well as within the St. Paul community.

West Publishing Co.

The lawyers of early St. Paul were a frustrated bunch. Nowhere could they find a regular and reliable source for decisions handed down by Minnesota judges. "Frontier" lawyers of Minnesota suffered a near black-out of information.

Enter John B. West, operator of a small bookstore that specialized in law books and legal forms near Kellogg and Wabasha streets in St. Paul. He quickly identified the need voiced by lawyers and, on October 21, 1876, began printing a weekly pamphlet called "The Syllabi." Within a year, Syllabi became an authoritative source of Minnesota legal information and it spawned a whole series of publications reporting opinions from all over the country.

Today, West Publishing of St. Paul is one of the oldest and largest publishers of legal information in the United States. Where West employees once handled handset type, they now transmit case information by computer to terminals in law offices all over the country. Where just a handful of people published a few dozen court opinions weekly, more than 2,000 West employees now collect, prepare and publish 40,000 cases each year.

The company's Key Number System — an efficient way to classify and index points of law — was considered an important growth catalyst for West when it was developed decades ago.

West Publishing has always been an important economic force and a downtown anchor for St. Paul. Always a major employer of St. Paul residents, West workers numbered 327 as early as 1887 and even held fast at 600 employees during the Depression. In fact, West is one of few companies that has had no layoffs of full-time employees for more than 46 years.

That security has led to employee longevity and one notable example is the late Homer P. Clark, early president of West. Mr. Clark worked 74 years for the company and retired at age 98 as honorary chairman of the West Publishing Board.

Over the years, West workers have demonstrated their loyalty to West and the city in a number of memorable ways. They fought floods, fires and became local Red Cross volunteers during the wars.

A   *Early shipping room scene*
     (Right) Publishing facility (1886)
B   *First edition of* The Syllabi, *Oct. 21, 1876*

A

B

244

Picture Credits

Pictures on the following pages are from the Minnesota Historical Society collections:
1, 2, 3d, 4a,c,d, 7, 8, 9, 10, 11, 12, 14, 15, 16, 17, 19, 20, 21, 22, 23, 26, 27, 30, 33, 34, 35, 36, 37, 39, 40a,b, 43, 44, 45, 46, 48a,c, 49, 52, 53, 56-57, 58, 59, 60, 61, 62, 64, 66, 68a, 72, 74, 75, 80, 81, 82, 90-91, 94, 95, 96, 97, 98, 99, 100, 101, 102, 104, 105, 106, 110, 111, 112, 113, 116, 117, 119, 121, 122, 123, 125c, 126, 127, 128b, 129, 133, 134, 135, 136-137, 138, 140, 141, 143, 146, 148, 151, 152.

Pictures on the following pages are from the *St. Paul Dispatch* and *Pioneer Press:*
90b, 108, 112, 114, 115, 118-119, 120, 124, 125b, 127b, 128a, 130, 131, 139, 142, 149, 150, 153, 154, 155, 156, 157, 158, 159, 160, 161, 162, 163, 164, 165, 166, 169, 170, 171, 172, 173.

Pictures on the following pages are from the Ramsey County Historical Society collections:
40c, 50-51, 54, 55, 68b, 70-71, 76-77, 78, 79, 84-85, 86, 87, 88, 92 *(Winter Carnival Souvenir Book)*, 92-93 *(Winter Carnival Souvenir Book*, 1887), 132, 144, Photographs on pages 24-25 by Paul Kuiper.

Color photographs on the following pages are by: Tom Roop, 175, 176, 177b, 178, 182, 183d, 185, 188b, 189a,b, 190; Cal Freedman, 177a, 180, 183c, 184b, 187b,d,e, 188c, 189c; Ron Geller, ii, vi, 186; Al Rung, 187c, 188a.

Other picture sources are as follows:
3c, 4b, Minneapolis Institute of Arts; 48b, private collection of Kenneth Carley; 69, 89, Minneapolis Public Library, Bromley Collection; 184a, City Planning Map.

Bibliography

A History of the City of St. Paul. St. Paul: Minnesota Historical Society, 1876.

Andrews, C.C. *History of St. Paul, Minnesota.* Syracuse: D. Mason, 1890. Part I, History of St. Paul; Part II, Biographical.

Atlas of Ramsey County, Minnesota. Compiled and drawn from official records and actual surveys by P.M. Dahl, C.E. Northwestern Map Publishing, 1898.

Atlas of St. Paul, Minnesota. Published by G.M. Hopkins, C.E.

Baker, Robert Orr. *The Muster Roll, A Biography of Fort Ripley, Minnesota.* St. Paul: H.M. Smyth Co., Inc., 1972.

Berthel, Mary Wheelhouse. *Horns of Thunder: The Life and Times of James M. Goodhue.* St. Paul: Minnesota Historical Society, 1948.

Blegen, Theodore C. *Minnesota: A History of the State.* Minneapolis: University of Minnesota Press, 1963.

Blue Book, Dual-City Directory. St. Paul: R.L. Polk & Co., 1907-8.

Board of Commissioners. *Minnesota in the Civil and Indian Wars, 1861-65.* St. Paul: Pioneer Press Co., 1899.

Brings, Lawrence M. *Minnesota Heritage.* Minneapolis: T.S. Denison and Co., Inc., 1960.

Brink, Carol. *The Twin Cities.* New York: Macmillan Co., 1961.

Brower, J.V. and Bushnell, D.I. *Memoirs of Explorations in the Basin of the Mississippi.* St. Paul: H.L. Collins Co., 1900. Vol. III, Mille Lacs and Vol. IV, Kathio.

Callender, John M. *New Light on Old Fort Snelling.* St. Paul: The Minnesota Historical Society, 1959, pp. 1-42.

Castle, Henry. *History of St. Paul and Vicinity.* Chicago and New York: Lewis Publishing Co., 1912, I, pp. 32-40; II, pp. 514-518; Vol. III.

City of St. Paul Atlas. St. Paul: Reuben H. Donnelley, 1892.

City Planning Board. *St. Paul Foreign-Born, Population Studies.* St. Paul: Minnesota Emergency Relief Administration, Project G2-F2-17, 1943.

Flandrau, Judge Charles E. *History of Minnesota.* St. Paul: E.W. Porter, 1900.

Flandrau, Grace. "St. Paul: The Personality of a City," *Minnesota History Quarterly Magazine*, XXII, (March, 1941), pp. 1-12.

Folwell, William Watts. *A History of Minnesota.* St. Paul: Minnesota Historical Society, 1921-I, 1924-II, 1926-III, 1929-IV.

Foster, Mary Dillon. *Who's Who Among Minnesota Women.* Mary Dillon Foster Publishing Co., 1924.

Fridley, Russell W. "The Beginnings of St. Paul," *Gopher Historian*, XIV, (Spring, 1960), pp.1-4.

Heilbron, Bertha L. *The Thirty-second State.* St. Paul: The Minnesota Historical Society, 1958.

Hennessy, W.B. *Past and Present of St. Paul, Minnesota.* Chicago: S.J. Clarke Publishing Co., 1906.

Hiebert, Gareth. "In St. Paul Where History Was Made," *Gopher Historian*, XIV, (Spring, 1960), pp. 8-11.

Holbrook, Franklin F. *St. Paul and Ramsey County in the War of 1917-1918.* (St. Paul, Ramsey County War Records Commission, 1929).

Jarchow, M.E., and Murchie, R.W. *Population Trends in Minnesota.* Minnesota: Experiment Station, Agricultural Bulletin 327, (May, 1936), pp. 23-39.

Lettermann, Edward J. *From Whole Log to No Log.* Minneapolis: Dillon Press, Inc., 1969.

Lindquist, Maude and Clark, James W. *Early Days and Ways in the Old Northwest.* New York: Scribner's, 1937.

Men of Minnesota, Minnesota Historical Company, 1902, 1915.

Moritz, W.F. *Atlas of the City of St. Paul.*

Morse, Edwin. *The Vanguard of American Volunteers.* New York: Scribner's, 1922.

Morse, Eric W. *Canoe Routes of the Voyageurs.* Royal Canadian Geographical Society, 1962.

Neill, Edward D. *History of the Minnesota Valley.* Minneapolis: North Star Publishing Company, 1882, pp. 263-274.

Neill, Edward D. *History of Ramsey County and the City of St. Paul.* Minneapolis: North Star Publishing Company, 1881.

Newson, T.M. *Pen Pictures of St. Paul.* St. Paul: published by the author, 1886.

Old Town Restoration, Inc. *Building the Future from Our Past: A Report on the Saint Paul Historic Hill District Planning Program.* St. Paul: Old Town Restorations, Inc. 1975.

One Hundred Years in the St. Paul Pioneer Press. St. Paul: The Pioneer Press, 1949.

Poatgieter, A. Hermina and Dunn, James Taylor. *Gopher Reader.* St. Paul: Minnesota Historical Society and Minnesota Statehood Centennial Commission, 1958.

Polk, R.W. *Little Sketches of Big Folks.* St. Paul, Minneapolis, Duluth: R.L. Polk and Company. 1907.

Pyle, Joseph Gilpin. *The Life of James J. Hill.* New York: Doubleday, 1917.

St. Paul City Directories. R.L. Polk and Company. 1886-67, 1932-59.

St. Paul Public Schools. *Essential Information About St. Paul.* St. Paul: Publication No. 90, 1962.

Schwartz, George M. and Thiel, George A. *Minnesota's Rocks and Waters, A Geological Story.* Minneapolis: University of Minnesota Press, 1954.

Sherman, John. *Music and Theater in Minnesota History.* William Van O'Connor, (ed.) Minneapolis: University of Minnesota Press, 1958.

Sibley, Henry Hastings. *Unfinished Autobiography of Henry H. Sibley.* Minneapolis: Voyageur Press, 1932.

Sickels, Alice L. *Around the World in St. Paul.* Minneapolis: University of Minnesota Press, United Lund Press, Inc., 1945, pp. 1-21.

Speer, Ray P. and Frost, Harry F. *Minnesota State Fair - The History and Heritage of 100 Years.* Argus, 1964.

Torbert, Donald R. *Century of Art and Architecture in Minnesota.* William Van O'Connor (ed.). Minneapolis: University of Minnesota Press, 1958.

Towne, Oliver (Gareth Hiebert). *Saint Paul is My Beat.* St. Paul: North Central Publishing Co., 1958.

Upham, Warren, *Minnesota Geographic Names, Origin and Historic Significances.* St. Paul: Minnesota Historical Society Collections, Vol. XVII, 1920.

West, Nathaniel. *The Ancestry, Life, and Times of Hon. Henry Hastings Sibley, L.L.D.* St. Paul: Pioneer Press, 1889.

Williams, J. Fletcher. *A History of the City of St. Paul.* St. Paul: Published by the Minnesota Historical Society, 1876.

Williams, J. Fletcher. *History of Ramsey County and the City of St. Paul.* Minneapolis: North Star Publishing Co., 1881.

Index/St. Paul History